Go back to The Garden

Ruth Scorey

Enlarge the place of your tent

(Isaiah 54:2)

First Published in Great Britain 2023

Copyright © Ruth Scorey, 2023

Ruth Scorey has asserted her right under the Copyright, Designs and Patents Act, 1988, to be identified as the Author of this work

For legal purposes the Acknowledgements and Endorsements on the next pages constitute an extension of this copyright page

All rights reserved. No part of this publication may be reproduced or transmitted in any form or by any means, electronic or mechanical, including photocopying, recording, or any information storage or retrieval system, without prior permission in writing from Ruth Scorey

ISBN: 9798399094540
Imprint: Independently published

Unless otherwise stated, all Scripture references are taken from the New International Version, British Text eBook Edition of the Bible: Hodder & Stoughton

Acknowledgements

I am indebted to:

Rev Ray Scorey, my encourager, husband and partner in time, without whom I couldn't have gone so deeply into the Lord;

Norfolk Healing Rooms for supporting and loving me and intrepidly exploring their own "gardens", as research for this manual;

Norfolk School of Prophets for allowing me to grow in the Spirit unimpeded, for bearing with me when I didn't get it right and for sharing their journeys into their own "gardens";

Glyn Jones, who has long supported and encouraged me in all things, including the prophetic, and supplied wise counsel for this manual;

Chris Wren James, for her inspiring and sage suggestions for this handbook, not to mention years of heart-expanding teaching and counselling;

***Jesus Ministry* conferences**, run by Christ Church Fulham, which introduced me to taking every thought captive, the divine exchange, exploring Heaven as a citizen and my first ever healing garden.

Endorsements

"What a fabulous and delightful book. Full of great healing activations, healing insights and breakthrough stories. This is poetic, lyric, with enough prophetic imagery to satisfy all the senses. Ruth is an insightful writer, with many lived experiences and years of walking alongside many on their healing journey. I highly recommend reading this."

Christine Wren James, Director, Life Streams International

"I have been using a prayer technique called "Going to the garden" for many years. I use it both personally and to teach other individuals and groups how to hear from God. I have found it to be a very helpful tool in leading some people, into the presence of God, who might otherwise find it difficult.

I have always said that prayer can be like jumping into a stream. When you first jump in, the sediment gets all stirred up, the water becomes cloudy and you can't see anything. But if you were to wait a moment, the sediment would settle and the water would become clear again. Likewise when we pray the enemy can fire in all sorts of distractions at the beginning, which can make us believe that we can't hear from God. However, if we were to linger just a little longer, the distractions would settle and we would find it much easier to hear from God.

Usually, when I do this exercise with people for the first time, I get them to imagine what I'm saying and I lead them into a garden with Jesus. This very simple but effective exercise helps them to linger long enough past the distractions. People who find this useful will then often go and use this whenever they like by themselves.

It's great to see that Ruth has put considerable thought into creating an actual theological framework around this beautiful concept. My hope and Prayer is that this book would bring other people into the Lord's presence and they would get to know Him better. I look forward to all the wonderful stories."

Dan Ward, Community Pastor, Sheringham Lighthouse Church

"I have had the privilege of knowing Ruth for a number of years and journeying with her as a friend, as well as leading prophetic training together. Ruth has an incredible capacity to remember Scripture and her captivating rendition of Song of Songs, by heart, is forever etched in my memory. One thing I value greatly is Ruth's integrity, openness and honesty. And this book clearly portrays these characteristics as she shares a number of personal testimonies to help you, the reader, to engage with the activations. This invitation to use your imagination—which is a beautiful gift from God—to explore *The Garden* of your heart will, I believe, help you to receive deeper layers of revelation of your own heart; drawing you into closer relationship with Him.

The step by step guidance with each activation gives practical advice without being restrictive. Each of our heart gardens are unique and so will be our journey.

The scriptural references provide solid grounding, as well as pictorial invitations to use our imagination with the Word of God.

This book can be read and worked through alone, with a friend, spouse or group and I would suggest journaling, so that you can revisit your encounters. I also would like to suggest that you may wish to go through the activations regularly and/or practise them as an annual exercise to expand and explore more of *The Garden* of your heart.

As I worked through the exercises myself, there was a mixture of laughter and healing tears, which served to water my own heart's garden. The Master Gardener showed me a number of weeds that needed uprooting, as well as seeds that we planted together and beautiful flowers and trees that grow as a result.

I have thoroughly enjoyed my own journey with this book and look forward to buying printed copies for myself and friends.

I pray that each of you will receive multiplied blessings as you read it."

__Michelle Smith, Seer, Prophet, Mentor, Spiritual advisor and Co-Leader of Glory Tribe with husband Rod__

Foreword

The condition of our hearts is vital. Why? Because so much of our life springs from the way our hearts respond to situations. The blueprint for all that God wants for us is already in our hearts, as are the plans for our future and the world's future. Western secularity prioritises the intellect, but God has a different way; He impresses things on our hearts, *before* it rises up into our intellect. We have to change the way we think and get used to negotiating in the Spirit.

Years ago, somebody once prayed over me, "God wants to enlarge your heart" and my spirit said yes to that. However, I wondered how that could actually come about, because there's not enough room in my chest for any more. Later, I asked the Lord about it and He told me to consider my heart like a garden. Then it all made sense. When you see your heart like a garden, it is much easier to see how it can grow beyond any conceived boundaries.

The title of this book comes out of an episode of life-threatening illness I had in late 2021, when I sought prayer support from Rev Paul Clift, the Lead Divisional Director for Healing Rooms Europe. When I telephoned, as arranged, Paul was outside gardening. When the phone rang, he felt God say "Ray is going to be fine. Go back to the garden." These were not only words I received fully for my healing, but the last five provided Ruth's book title. Going back to *The Garden* of our hearts is all about enlarging our experience and understanding of our original design in God and His promises to us for life, health and wholeness.

Rev Ray Scorey

Introduction

At my ordination into Healing Rooms Ministries, at the Spokane headquarters in 2016, Lori Taylor from Santa Marie Healing Rooms felt the Lord repeatedly say over me: "The book! The book! The book! The book! The book!" It was clear to us both that I had a book to write, although neither of us knew what kind of book it might be at that time; but here it is.

I have faithfully kept a prayer diary since 2011, when I began to journal my quiet times with the Lord every day. This made me realise that God is speaking to us all the time, whether we are listening to Him or not. Then, in 2012, I attended my second *Jesus Ministry* conference at Christ Church Fulham in London. There, we all did a short individual meditation on Revelation 4. So remarkable was that experience, that I phoned Ray, my husband to be, to tell him all about it; "Did you know that the sea of glass tinkles? And do you know why it tinkles? Because there are diamonds in the surf!"

My imagination had connected me with the Word of God in such a way that it brought Heaven alive and made it somehow *more* than three dimensional. Scripture makes it clear that Heaven is very much *al fresco*—outdoors—and I realised that not only is Heaven a giant garden but it also has a mind and life all of its own; the mind and life of Christ.

Since then, we have both experienced a deepening understanding of what *The Garden* of our hearts might be. I hope this manual will help you too to experience the very real presence and healing of God in *The Garden* of your own heart.

This manual is unashamedly scattered with Bible references. They are strong rungs on the ladder to heavenly understanding. I have not always taken God at His Word and, in the past, have taken Scripture with large pinches of salt. But because God is good all the time, He is utterly trustworthy and it is right to trust what is written in the Bible; it is God-breathed (2 Timothy 3:16) and written through people trained in the art of listening to Him. Because the greatest commandments in the Bible are to love God and to love others, reading Scripture through the lens of love will always help us better understand the meaning of our creator.

Rev Ruth Scorey

My Soul is a House
By El Gruer

My soul is a house,
My heart is a garden,
My Spirit is an ocean,
My mind is a field.

My soul is Your house,
My heart is Your garden,
My spirit is Your ocean,
My mind is Your field.

You live in the house,
You walk in the garden,
You sail on the ocean,
You dance in the field.

My soul is Your house,
My heart is Your garden,
My spirit is Your ocean,
My mind is Your field.

Always Yours.

Contents

Chapter 1	**The Garden of our Hearts**	Page 1
	The Seeker's Prayer	Page 16
Chapter 2	**Imagination as a Safe Gardening Tool**	Page 17
Chapter 3	**The Garden: A Meeting of Two Minds**	Page 25
	Activation 1: Concrete thinking	Page 26
	Activation 2: Abstract thinking	Page 27
	Activation 3: Litmus test for your imagination	Page 30
	Activation 4: Kick starting your imagination	Page 34
	Activation 5: Lectio divina: the first garden	Page 36
Chapter 4	**Exploring The Garden**	Page 37
	Activation 6: Being a citizen of Heaven	Page 39
	Activation 7: The ten-minute garden	Page 42
Chapter 5	**Intimacy and The Garden**	Page 49
	Activation 8: Becoming the Bride	Page 51
	Activation 9: Drawing parallels from Song of Songs	Page 58
	Activation 10: For married couples	Page 59
Chapter 6	**The Garden in Times of Trouble**	Page 61
	Activation 11: Experiencing Psalm 23	Page 63
	Activation 12: Making Psalm 23 personal	Page 65
Chapter 7	**The Ever Expanding Garden**	Page 73
Chapter 8	**Others' Experiences of The Garden**	Page 79
Chapter 9	**The Garden as a Ministry Tool for Facilitators and Ministers**	Page 87
Chapter 10	**Prayers for Inner Healing**	Page 105
	Dealing with unhealthy soul ties	Page 105
	Dealing with fear, shock and trauma	Page 108
	Dealing with unforgiveness	Page 110
	Dealing with the occult	Page 111
	How to keep your healing	Page 115
	Where to get further help	Page 117
APPENDIX 1	**A Bible Full of Garden Imagery**	Page 119
APPENDIX 2	**Key to Elements of Song of Songs**	Page 125
APPENDIX 3	**Fifteen Promises of God**	Page 139
Bibliography	**& Recommended Reading**	Page 141
Index		Page 143

Chapter 1

The Garden of our Hearts

'Now the Lord God had planted a garden in the east, in Eden; and there He put the man He had formed.'
(Genesis 2:8)

'He has also set eternity in the human heart.'
(Ecclesiastes 3:11)

This chapter provides a scriptural foundation for *The Garden* of our hearts, building a firm theological basis for the concept of our hearts as spiritual gardens.

What is *The Garden*?

You may be wondering why I have called this manual *Go back to The Garden*. What garden am I talking about? Where on Earth is it and why should we go back to it?

Just imagine being able to walk in a beautiful garden, for ten minutes each day, as part of your daily "quiet time". Picture the rich green grass sweeping away before you, across an estate of pleasant and gently rolling land. There is a beautiful lake, the sun sparkling on the still waters. A picnic awaits you. All your favourite things to eat are set out on a red gingham cloth, carefully arranged on the grass. It is summer and the trees are in full leaf, providing welcome coolness and shade. Jesus is sitting beside the feast, looking at you and waiting for you to join Him. You don't know how long He's been there, but He is not impatient. He enjoys watching you as you approach and you feel excitement and joy rising up in you, as you near the man who is not only God but your very best friend. You don't know exactly what will be said or what will happen, but you do know that here is a place where every bit of you is not only welcome and celebrated, but very, very safe. Your heart swells as you approach the love of your life.

When you spend time imagining this garden, with Jesus in it, you discover that there are more gardens to explore: woodlands, waterfalls, seaside, formal gardens with fountains, mountains, a beautiful mansion, a palace and, you soon begin to realise, that there is always more. When you are there, Jesus shows you things. You talk, play or simply gaze into each other's faces. Everything carries meaning and you never know how long you will stay in any particular part of the garden. You never want to forget what you find and learn there, so you constantly write down everything in your journal. When you return from these forays, you often read and re-read your notes and realise it is all making you bigger on the inside than you were before.

After ten minutes each day, you'll have spent the heavenly equivalent of nearly seven years walking with God, because 'with the Lord a day is like a thousand years' (2 Peter 3:8). In that short ten minutes you find that He does 'immeasurably more [in you and with you] than [you could possibly] ask or imagine' (Ephesians 3:20). Each day becomes a journey, a love story and a joy in these precious and heavenly short ten minutes, in which you become aware that you are being 'taught by the Lord' (Isaiah 54:13).

The Garden of our heart is a heavenly place to go to, in our "sanctified or faith imagination"; that is, our mind's eye when it is submitted to God. Journeys to *The Garden* are all about being in the presence of the Lord, in order to interact with Him. They can be inspired directly by Scripture or are forays of discovery in which Jesus, 'the Word' (John 1:1), makes Himself known to us in a very immediate sense. Each one of us has the ability to walk with the Lord in *The Garden* of our hearts, 'in the cool of the day' (Genesis 3:8).

Simply put, *The Garden*:

- is spiritual and scriptural territory to be inhabited, explored and journeyed through by the people of God;
- is deeply connected to our God-given spiritual identity, inheritance and purpose in Christ;
- can be accessed using our mind's eye, through a process of visualisation, which incorporates our spiritual senses, making it an immersive experience in heavenly realms;
- is at once surrendered, as well as connected to the mind of Christ;
- is imbued with the presence of God and helps us to build our relationship with Him;
- is a safe place to linger with the Lord in Godly contemplation;
- is a place of spiritual revelation, insight, healing, renewal, adventure and learning.

The purpose of going to *The Garden* is manifold and will be explored more fully throughout this manual. Broadly speaking, it is to delve into the spiritual territory of our heart; the new heart that God placed within us when we were born again, as promised in Ezekiel 36:26. Our Heavenly Father didn't accomplish this organ transplant as might be performed by hospital surgeons. Rather, our spiritual heart was transplanted spiritually at the moment we invited Christ to dwell in our heart through faith, as described in Ephesians 3:17. So our spiritual heart is the core of our being, that is 'renewed day by day' (2 Corinthians 4:16), by the life force of Heaven. This process of renewal and restoration is our heavenly inheritance; ours to enjoy forever, despite our outward, physical body wasting away.

Where is Heaven?
Christians have long spoken of "going to Heaven" when they die, despite Jesus saying that 'the Kingdom of God has come upon us' (Luke 11:20) and 'is in your midst' (Luke 17:21). This manual makes it clear that we are not just mortal beings waiting to die and go to Heaven. Rather, Heaven is already here and may be received by any heart open to welcoming it in. We're not waiting to get into Heaven, but enjoying Heaven getting into us. And where the Kingdom of Heaven is, there is God; to all intents and purposes 'Heaven *is* Him' (Johnson, 2022). Jesus died not only so that His Holy Spirit could fill us, but that we might have complete communion with the full trinity of God, as Jesus describes in John 17:20-23.

When we accept Christ as our Saviour and Healer, we become a new creation; our outer shell may be mortal, but we now have an eternal core. Indeed, God has 'set eternity in the human heart' (Ecclesiastes 3:11), just waiting to be activated. So while our bodies may well be as frail as 'jars of clay' (2 Corinthians 4:7), we are full of heavenly treasure; awaiting discovery so it can be multiplied and given away. So the Kingdom is in our hearts and Heaven starts now.

Where Heaven and *The Garden* meet:
And this is where *The Garden* meets the heart, because the heart is where Heaven resides. Consequently, there are a number of garden scriptures connecting Heaven and the human heart. The Parable of the Sower in Mark 4:3-20 is just one example; the Word of God is like seed that falls to the ground, growing well in the good soil of those who receive it. That soil represents the heart, for 'it is with your heart that you believe' (Romans 10:10). So, those who receive the Word of God germinate it in their hearts, just as if seed were planted in a garden. In Isaiah 61:11 this garden of the heart causes 'seeds to grow', enabling a mighty crop to spring up there, as The Parable of the Sower affirms. Thus, Jesus is the Word, the Word is like seed and our hearts are like soil. Subsequently, a garden grows up, as we develop deeper understanding of Jesus, Father God and the Holy Spirit.

Jesus is the Word, the Word seed and our hearts soil
(Painting of Jesus by the late Sarah McCrum)

There is one master key to open the door to *The Garden* and that is the cross. When we believe, accept and celebrate what Jesus did on the cross for us, we metaphorically insert a key into the keyhole of our heart, in ord-

The cross is the key to our heart

er to open "the door" to our heart as a garden. Once we open that door, we invite our Father in Heaven to be 'The Gardener' (John 15:1) of our heart, Jesus to be 'our beloved' (Song of Songs 2:3) and Holy Spirit to be the revealer of 'the deep things of God' (1 Corinthians 2:10), as well as our protector, teacher and counsellor as promised in Psalm 32:7-8.

When we see our heart as a garden, the act of taking communion develops deeper meaning; the bread becomes life-giving seed and the wine revitalizing rain. Eating Jesus' "body" and drinking His "blood" is a work of sowing and watering. It actively invites The Gardener of our hearts to grow our awareness of the vast and many-splendoured garden planted there. Because Jesus is the 'Bread of Life' (John 6:35) and His life 'is in [His] blood' (Leviticus 17:11), it's not just a ritual; it's life transforming.

The Garden is within

The first garden on Earth was the Garden of Eden and this manual will explain how we, as Christians, can not only go *back* to this original garden but discover many other gardens of God's Kingdom. The lovely oneness with God, which Adam and Eve enjoyed in Eden before The Fall, has been regained for us by what Christ did on the cross. And because the cross has given us access to Heaven in our hearts, we also have access not only to that original garden, but to the whole estate of Heaven. As 'our citizenship is in Heaven' (Philippians 3:20), it's about time we got to know our spiritual homeland; after all, it's our inheritance. We have heavenly real estate simply waiting to be discovered by us and it's our heart that is the sacred site in which such spiritual breakthrough takes place.

Body, soul and spirit:
Because our heart corresponds to what we also call our spirit, it's useful to know how this relates to the other two parts that incorporate our make-up; those of body and soul.

BODY:
As already mentioned, our physical body is mortal and obviously consists of our flesh: brain, limbs, organs and bones. The brain is simply hardware, rather than the centre of our being, because when the brain dies our spirits live on.

SOUL:
It's helpful to make a distinction between the soul and the spirit, rather than seeing these terms as interchangeable. Hebrews 4:12 certainly makes a distinction between the two concepts, the word of God penetrating 'even to dividing soul and spirit'. While the soul is not physical, it finds its expression through being in a physical body. It is an assortment of the conscious and subconscious mind, emotions and the will. Humanism, which places people at the centre of life on Earth, depends on reason to live well. However, once Holy Spirit has in-filled a person, the soul's mental powers have to submit to God or forever be in direct opposition to Him. This doesn't mean we give up our ability to think and problem solve. It just means that our brain is not our God. Because God's 'thoughts are not [our] thoughts' (Isaiah 55:8), submitting our intellect to God is a big key to activating our ability to tune into His thoughts. When we learn to think like God thinks, then is the beginning of bringing Heaven down to Earth.

SPIRIT:
At our core is our spirit which, when coupled with God, is our true identity and our real eternal being. Without God, our spirits are like bereft stumps, acting like antennae searching for that *something* to complete us. Many people use this internal signal to search for the true meaning of life, but may instead connect with other "powers" along the way; New Ageism for example, which taps into power without seeking to know who is behind it. But Jesus makes it clear that there is only one true meaning to life and that's Him; He is 'the way, the truth and the life' (John 14:6) and He is the only way to reattach ourselves to God. Other ways may connect to other gods or other supernatural forces, but they are not the one true God.

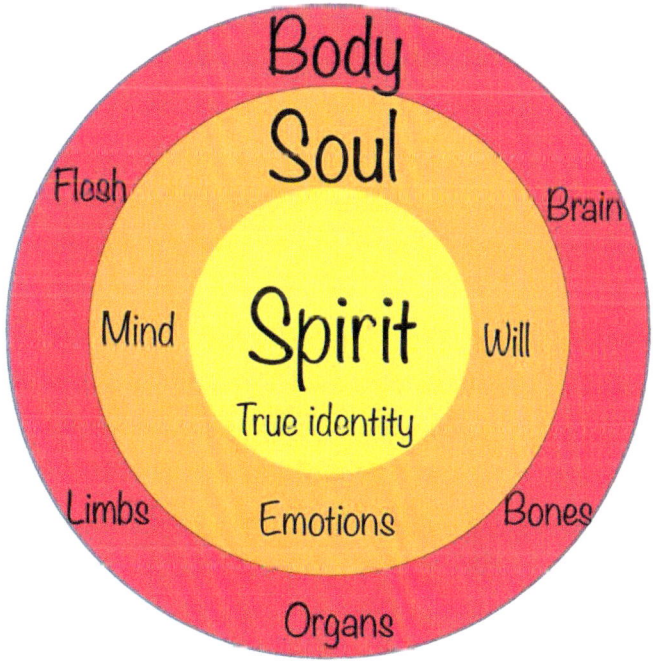

We are made up of three parts: body, soul and spirit

We were never designed to live without our Creator, but *The Fall* in Eden created a divide between people and their Maker. Instead of opting for God and choosing life, in Genesis 3:1-7, Adam and Eve chose to have knowledge; with its penalty of death. Thus, they chose to live their lives independently of God, relinquishing access to the One who *is* life, the author of life and life in all its fullness. And so death was brought into the world that day. It took Jesus' death on the cross, an act of immense love and sacrifice, to pay the price for the most costly decision on earth and re-open our way back to our Heavenly Father. It took the coming of Holy Spirit to restore people back to their original design, which gives us the ability to know God personally, as well as to learn the ways of Heaven.

Once reconnected to The Father, through Jesus and Holy Spirit, we are a new creation. Rather like stacking dolls, we are wonderfully triple nested, one inside the other; Holy Spirit in us, us in Jesus and Jesus in The Father. This rather over-simplifies something which is a paradox and a mystery, but it does go some way to explaining what Jesus envisaged in His prayer in John 17:20-23, when He longed to see us brought to complete unity with God; us dwelling in Him and He in us. The mystery is that, while we have Holy Spirit in us, this Holy Spirit also ushers in the Spirit of Jesus. This allows Christ to be 'formed in [us]' (Galatians 4:19), as He dwells in our hearts through faith. Even more enigmatically, because Jesus is in the Father as the Father is in Him (John 14:11), it follows on that if we have Jesus in us we also have the Father.

Holy Spirit in us, us in Jesus and Jesus in the Father

So, we are fully grafted into the True Vine of God; completely connected to Him, with all His goodness flowing through our veins. This is surely what Luke 17:20-21 means, in The Passion Translation (2020), when he says that 'God's Kingdom realm is already expanding within some of you', for the Kingdom of God is wherever God is; Father, Son and Holy Spirit. This Trinity of God is beautifully inter-dependent; Holy Spirit, sent by the Father, 'intercedes for us in accordance with the will of God' (Romans 8:27), and Jesus does 'only what He sees His Father doing' (John 5:19). This is what we are invited to be part of and one with. Somehow, going to *The Garden* makes this eternal knot much simpler to comprehend. It is an easily accessible place within our own spirit, to meet with God in order to achieve our heavenly destiny, i.e. what we were actually born for. *The Garden* is less of an academic exercise and more about simply experiencing God's presence.

The self as a mirror of the Trinity:
The trinity of self—body, soul and spirit—rather beautifully mirrors the Trinity of God, in which Father, Son and Holy Spirit work in heavenly unison. To be in His likeness, our body, soul and spirit also need to be unified in God, to avoid the feeling that things are not quite right within us. Bringing everything into alignment with God creates a core of wellbeing and *The Garden* is a useful device in this endeavour, as it is an environment where all three parts of us can meet all three parts of God. I know, through my involvement with Healing Rooms, that both physical and mental health are deeply connected to spiritual health. It's good to care for our bodies and keep our minds sharp and positive, but caring for our spiritual wellbeing is paramount. Spiritual health is Jesus' main message. When we get that, we get everything.

New creations in Christ:
In Colossians 3:3, Paul makes it clear that our old self dies once we have found our true identity, which is 'hidden with Christ in God'. This means that our once independent soul surrenders control to the rightful captain of our lives and our spirit comes into its true inheritance, as it unites with God. You have to give up the life you've built for yourself, in order to gain the better life found in Jesus, as intimated in Matthew 10:39. Full-immersion baptism is a symbol of this; the descent beneath the water represents dying to a life centred around self and the subsequent resurfacing signifies rebirth into a new life, with Jesus at the heart.

Once the old self has died, just as an infant must develop and mature to adulthood, it's important for our new self to start growing in God and create room for God to grow in us. Derek Prince (2013) asserts that it is vital for Christians to know *how* to be led by Holy Spirit, in order to mature and not 'remain perpetual infants'. Because *The Garden* is Spirit led, it being His domain, going there is one way to be proactive in seeking out the Lord for spiritual growth. When we submit our faith imagination to Him, we give Him full permission to lead us to those places in which we most need to develop, making *The Garden* a place in which to flourish.

The Garden as interactive space:

The Garden is a place where we co-operate with God, in order to experience development. Such advancement necessitates a treasure-seeking approach, as in Proverbs 2:1-5, in which we are called to search the thoughts of God as people seeking for silver: searching; digging; extracting and refining. Indeed the lives of our biblical forebears make it clear that our lives and the lives of others depend on it. We were never meant to simply take the Bible as read, but to dig for the Lord's multi-dimensional spiritual wisdom and understanding. After all, Heaven is more real than what we see with our limited earthly vision; as 2 Corinthians 4:18 explains, what we see with our eyes will pass away, but the things of God are eternal.

With the Father overseeing our progress, *The Garden* is safe space in which the children of God can play. God delights in getting us involved in what He's doing there, so *The Garden* is interactive space to be explored in the presence of the one who is the lover of our soul. And it's safe because everything in *The Garden* is focused on Him; on His mind and His heart, which are always good. Also, main control over what we see in *The Garden* belongs to God and not to us and the only person who is all powerful in *The Garden* is Him; not us. If there is weeding to be done there, it is done by our Heavenly Father, who is The Gardener; and a gentle one at that.

As we work together with the Lord, we discover *The Garden* is actual spiritual territory and our forays become a divine pursuit. The interaction between our surrendered imagination and the leading of Holy Spirit creates a kind of heavenly "tardis" within us, in which we are bigger on the inside than we look on the outside.

Relational learning:

Graham Cooke (2022) calls this kind of heavenly discovery 'relational learning', in which we 'think with our heart and learn from inside God's heart, inside our own heart; so we begin to learn from the inside to the outside'. Graham goes on to say that truth, wisdom and revelation first require a heart response, followed by focused thinking, in order to upgrade our perspective of God and who we are in Him. This is where one thought leads to another and another until we discover that we are enlarging the territory of our hearts and our minds, through the mind of Christ. Similarly, *The Garden* becomes heavenly territory in which to repeatedly explore God's heart and receive deeper revelation of Him. There we experience His presence in our hearts, stimulating heavenly thoughts that change us inside out; not only upgrading our experience of God but tooling us up to impact the world around us.

Childlike trust and mystery:
The Garden requires an attitude of childlikeness in order to access the treasure within. Bill Johnson (2022) says some aspects of the Kingdom can only be learned through a combination of childlike trust and mystery. In this vein, *The Garden* requires us to have an approach that is inquisitive, excited and teachable, with the capacity to appreciate the notion that mystery involves revelation which can't always be fully comprehended. With each journey into *The Garden*, we get more understanding of God and of our identity in Him. So *The Garden* offers a way of building up our 'treasures in Heaven' (Matthew 6:20).

What *The Garden* is not:
While it is true that *The Garden* is a catalyst for contemplation, it is neither an anonymous mystic tool nor a New Age meditation garden; it is neither a form of astral projection, nor is it a foray delving into the labyrinth of our minds or doorways of perception. Just because these things exist, does not mean we must run a mile from using our imagination. If we don't recognise that all counterfeits have their true original—otherwise they wouldn't be counterfeits—then we risk throwing out the baby with the bath water; the baby being true spiritual revelation in a true spiritual garden. With the One True God in us, we have the God-given ability to identify the wolf in sheep's clothing; because God's sheep know and 'listen to His voice' (John 10:27), we recognise what doesn't come from Him. So we have no need to be afraid of being swindled by *The Garden*. The true Godly garden is full of lots of good spiritual fruit and fear and suspicion are not among them.

With regard to the use of gardens in other religions, there may be some similarities to *The Garden* of our hearts, but there are also essential differences. The biggest difference is that Jesus will always be in *The Garden*, in one form or another, as long as it is surrendered to Him. In contrast, Zen Buddhism is more a philosophy than a religion. It considers the imagined garden as representing the flow of eternal life through the mystery of time, in the absence of a deity. While *The Garden* of the sanctified imagination is very much about the flowing of eternal life, the truth is that this eternal life emanates from the One who *is* the actual Lord of Time. In many ways He is undeniably a mystery, but He invites us to become acquainted with Him in all His ways, as He is acquainted with us in all of ours. *The Garden*, surrendered to God, is an excellent place to do this. When we choose to dwell in Him and allow Him to live in us, it is as if we enter the Garden of Eden anew to walk with Him there, allowing His eternal life to flow in, through and out of us.

What happens when meditation is not surrendered to God:
Many religions use meditation, Christianity included. Meditation in itself is not harmful; mindfulness is a Buddhist technique which is widely used in health care and which trains the mind to be present, calm and without judgement. However, Christian meditation will always place Jesus at the centre. Garden imagery is used in a number of other religions, e.g. Shamanism and Druidism, as a meditative device to explore the internal landscape of the mind, sometimes referred to as the "inner grove". But while this may seem like an innocent self-help tool, whatever is not rooted in Jesus tends to attract our invisible enemy, who is always trying to get between us and God. When Druids see "obliging" gnomes and pixies in their inner groves, the spiritual forces at work there are not aligned to the Lord; we can say this with absolute certainty, because there are no gnomes or pixies in the Bible. So, we need to be aware that any place not surrendered to God can attract enemy factions that savour deception as a form of insidious attack.

Moreover, in the ungodly garden, the ego is often the self-elected ruler there and this can be very attractive to "lost souls" seeking security through their own self-imposed control. Nevertheless, people were never designed to live without God and certainly not to *be* God; actually that was and is beelzebub's[i] desire for himself and he longs for us to emulate him. In *The Garden* of our hearts, God is in charge and our true life and freedom come from surrendering everything to Him in that place.

Because satan[ii] also had access to the original biblical garden, it is absolutely vital that we ensure that *The Garden* of our own heart is fully surrendered to God. If we do not invite Jesus to be there with us and Holy Spirit to guide us, it is entirely possible that *The Garden* may become a place of spiritual invasion or remain contaminated with unholy elements of other previous belief systems. Any part of us that is not surrendered to God is easily commandeered by the enemy, who is like a 'roaring lion looking for someone to devour' (1 Peter 5:8).

If you do experience ungodly elements in your garden, despite having carefully submitted everything to God, be encouraged and keep your eyes on Jesus there. We all have baggage, in the form of obstructive personal responses resulting from past hurts; we are creatures of habit, with a tendency to fall back on previously learned patterns of thinking. 'The Spirit is willing but the flesh is weak' (Matthew 26:41) and old inclinations can die hard.

However, *The Garden* is an ideal place for the Lord to deal with these things. Christine Wren James (2014) writes:

> *'God wants to release us from our shame into His glory and boldness. His desire is to redeem the entire person and He doesn't leave out any "bits". In Matthew Chapter 13 Jesus speaks of finding something precious that is hidden in a field and selling everything to purchase that field. In a sense, we are the field and God has always known the treasure that we carry that is hidden. He buys the whole field, complete with dead trees, weeds and rocks and broken down walls, because He sees the incredible treasure in this field. YOU.'*

All darkness must flee in God's presence and intimacy with the Lord drives out shadows, because His 'perfect love drives our fear' (I John 4:18). In 1 John 4:8, love personifies God even more than fear embodies satan[ii] and we always have 'the victory through our Lord Jesus Christ' (1 Corinthians 15:57). With these things in mind, as with all prayer, we first commit ourselves to God before entering *The Garden*. Then we enter with childlike trust and a teachable attitude. When we cross a bridge from one side to the other, we leave behind what's gone before to embrace the new. In this way, *The Garden* helps us let go of our old, dead self and embrace the new creation we really are.

We cross a bridge to the new self, leaving the old self behind

The Garden and our true identity:

It can take a life time of learning how to watch and pray in the Spirit, in order to ensure that our "soulishness" remains dead and buried; enabling us to leave behind our old self, with all its hankerings and insecurities of false identity. While some people can change completely in a flash at conversion, most of us require the drip-by-drip method of 'being transformed into His image with ever increasing glory' (2 Corinthians 3:18). Heaven is within us, but it will take eternity to fully grasp. Nevertheless, we can live life in all its fullness, as God intended, by embracing the one in whom our true identity lies; Jesus. Happily, *The Garden* is a place which is exceptionally good at enabling this process of becoming who we were designed to be. With every visit to *The Garden*, the old self diminishes as the true identity expands.

The rest is yet to come:

This manual explores what it takes to enter *The Garden*, presents different types of scriptural gardens and explains various features of and applications for *The Garden*. There are a number of testimonies of those who have accessed *The Garden* of their own hearts. Throughout, there are activations to help you 'taste and see that the Lord is good' (Psalm 34:8) in *The Garden* of your own heart and that it is a blessing to take refuge in Him there. It is a good idea to do the activations as they come up, so that you start to engage with what God has planted in you from the off. Then, as the chapters expand, so will your experience and understanding of *The Garden.*

Saying 'yes' to God:

Graham Cooke (2016) writes that God is not looking at you to see what's wrong with you; He's looking at you to see 'what's missing of your experience of Him'. And Richard Rohr (2003) writes 'God doesn't look at our faults, but at the places in us that are trying to say "yes".

If you have never said "yes" to God, consider saying out loud the seeker's prayer overleaf, before reading the rest of this manual.

The Seeker's Prayer:

(Say aloud)

Dear Father God, King of the universe and Maker of all, thank You that you love me and know me. Thank You that you chose me before the creation of the world. Thank You that You know the plans You have for me; plans to prosper me and not to harm me, plans to give me hope and a future. Thank You that You love me just as I am and meet me exactly where You find me.

I accept that the word 'sin' refers to anything that doesn't put You first and am sorry for any sin in my life. I renounce any involvement I have had in the past with the occult or spiritual guides other than You and Your Holy Spirit. Please forgive me for anything I have said, thought or done, whether knowingly or accidentally, which has been less about You and more about me or anything that is in opposition to You.

Thank you that you accept me as I am because, by dying on the cross and rising from the dead, Jesus paid the price that was on my head. Thank You that You made a way for me to reconnect my spirit with You, my Maker, to become a cleansed, saved, healed and whole child of God, as well as an inheritor of Heaven from this day forward. Thank you that you do not condemn me, but only have great love and compassion for me.

I now choose to open the door of my heart and say, 'Jesus, come into my heart and fill me with Your Holy Spirit, that I may walk with You; to discover Your ways, to learn to love You and be loved by You, to come to know You and to make You known.

Happy Re-Birthday!

Now sign and date below, so that in the years to come you can celebrate the anniversary of starting your new life in Christ:

Signed: ....

Date: ....

Chapter 2

Imagination as a Safe Gardening Tool

'Let my beloved come into His garden.'
(Song of Songs 4:16)

This chapter lays out a scriptural foundation for the use of the imagination as safe spiritual practice. It aims to reassure those, who are cautious about choosing to use the imagination as a means of communicating with God.

To see *The Garden* in the mind's eye and experience the transformational journey of regularly going there, we need to use a God-given "garden tool": our imagination. In other words, to see *The Garden* of our heart, we first have to "open" the eyes of our heart; as intimated by Ephesians 1:18. This involves a visualisation process, which unites our own natural concepts with God's heavenly thoughts; consequently awakening our spiritual senses. With God in us and us in God, we are a kind of composite, in which the earthly and the Godly merge to form a new creation. In this dynamic bonding, when we weave the pictures of our mind's eye together with spiritual territory, we create something familiar, yet more vibrant and powerful. The result brings insight and understanding to spiritual things beyond our earthly abilities. In Chapters 3-6 there are a number of activations to whet your imagination. But first, it will be established how and why the imaginative power of our mind is required to enter *The Garden*.

The Garden as a tool for renewing the mind:

In Romans 12:2 Paul urges us to 'be transformed by the renewing of [our] mind'. *The Garden* is essentially a classroom for the children of God to renew their minds and grow in His presence. There are, of course, many ways to be renewed on the inside, e.g. reading and meditating on the Bible, learning Scripture, praise, worship, prayer, fellowship with other Christians, being still in the presence of God, enjoying God's natural creation etc. Most Christians will do some, all and more of these things regularly week by week and most build a "quiet time" into their daily lives to focus on the Word of God. 'The Word is alive and active' (Hebrews 4:12), so when we interact with it we are actually connecting with a person; Jesus.

When we enter *The Garden*, we bring what we know to a place that allows us to see things from God's perspective. No matter how much or how little we know of Scripture, because He *is* the Word, Jesus meets us exactly where we are on our faith journey and teaches us from that point. His ways are not our ways and, in *The Garden*, His methods tend to be surprising, tender and delightful. In this way, *The Garden* is like a "three-dimensional canvas" on which The Word is painted, to communicate God's truth and revelation to us. It's a place where we can discover who we truly are in Him and His good plans for our lives.

As already established, to see the Kingdom of God and to build relationship with Him we are called to be childlike. Indeed, Matthew 18:3 asserts that we simply can't enter the Kingdom of God unless we become like little children. This takes quite a lot of humility; proactively submitting our own take on things, to willingly open ourselves up to hear and learn things from God's perspective and embrace the mystery. This throwing-off of self makes it possible for us to be taught by the Lord and *The Garden* facilitates this process. Bill Johnson describes embracing mystery as a transaction; as we relinquish self, God gives us more. It's like the seed, in John 12:24, that falls into the ground and dies in order to multiply. This is not about mortal death, but a process of dying to the old self in order to inherit the true self.

Imagination as a tool for student-centred learning in *The Garden*:
Graham Cooke (2007) writes:

> *'[God's] dreams for us are so big, only a creative imagination may access it. The Holy Spirit increases our experience constantly, pulling us into a greater place of personal trust and outrageous faith and teaching us to move beyond mere logic and reason to a place where we can dwell in the bigness of God's calling and not be minimised or disenfranchised by our obvious humanity!'*

The value of the gift of imagination is often underestimated; what appears to be a small playful step can be a giant leap in our journey towards God. There are a number of advantages to actively engaging our imagination to enter *The Garden*, when renewing our minds:

- Firstly, all learning in *The Garden* is individually catered for each one of us, progressing us through steps and stages of ever increasing levels of knowledge and wisdom, which are all designed to meet our own particular needs;
- Secondly, *The Garden* is a place of active encounter, where learning takes place first hand through experience and relationship with the Lord;
- Thirdly, *The Garden* blends the heavenly with the familiar, which facilitates the journey through the Kingdom's extraordinary approach to life;
- Fourthly, gardens are places of pleasure, so the beauty of *The Garden* makes learning a joyful experience.

This kind of connecting with Heaven not only brings with it a deep-seated and satisfying knowledge of God, but also fosters transformative self worth.

Why we shouldn't be afraid of using our imagination:

Because a number of Bible translations of 2 Corinthians 10:5 speak of the need to cast down imagination, some Christians have misunderstood Paul's directive and assume that it means that no Christian should ever imagine anything. This is a rather sad mistake to make, because Paul is not referring to our creative ability to visualise and dream good things. The NIV writes:

> *'We demolish arguments and every pretension that sets itself up against the knowledge of God, and we take captive every thought to make it obedient to Christ.'*

Meanwhile, The Passion Translation (2020) says this:

> *'We can demolish every deceptive fantasy, every arrogant attitude that is raised up in defiance of the true knowledge of God.'*

So Paul is speaking about those deceitful fabrications and thoughts that contradict God's truth. So it's all about renewing our mind and not about quashing creativity. As David Watson (cited in Huggett 1996) used to say, 'the antidote to misuse and abuse is not no use but right use'.

Then again, other Christians fear the imagination on the assumption that it is an instrument with which we disobey the scriptural directives telling us not to add or take away anything from the Bible. But, when used with God at the centre, the imagination simply deepens our understanding of His Word. This is not about redacting from or adding to the accepted canon of Scripture, but about opening our spiritual eyes to receive more insight and truth from what is written on the page. It does not fly in the face of Scripture, but brings heavenly inspiration to, through and by the Word.

When our imagination is surrendered to God, it can be a very useful tool for searching Him out. For years the Jesuits have used visualisation and imagination, to respond in a deeply-felt personal way to scenes from the life of Christ. Also, Rabbi Jason Sobel (2023) explains that Jews continue to use the age-old method of "midrash", to re-imagine biblical texts in order to interpret, elaborate, fill in gaps and answer unexplained questions. In this way, the imagination becomes a heavenly tool when used for heavenly purposes.

The main message here is that our imagination does not, by its nature, inherently oppose God. We have to remember that we are made by a good God, who made us in His image (Genesis 1:26-27). And God must surely have His own imagination. After all, He chose us '*before* the creation of the world' (Ephesians 1:4), before we were even born. This is because He has that amazing ability to call 'into being things that were not' (Romans 4:17); picturing us in His mind before life on Earth even began. Essentially, He dreamed us in order to be able to choose us, before He 'knit [us] together in [our] mother's womb' (Psalm 139:13).

It must surely follow that, as His children, we have inherited God's ability to dream. Our faith imagination enables us to picture the impossible and bring the heavenly down to Earth. This is essentially what The Lord's Prayer is getting at. This isn't about making something happen by the force of the mind; it is about bringing down the heavenly, by allowing our mind the freedom to agree with the mind of God. So when our thoughts align with His, 'all things are possible' (Matthew 19:26).

Choosing how to think and imagine:
We all have a choice how to use our imagination and it is an act of daily obedience to bring our imagination into line with God and away from anything ungodly. Original choice was always heavenly. We know this because God did it first, by choosing us before the beginning of time.

But choice was also one of the first tests mankind had to face. As already explained in Chapter 1, Adam and Eve chose knowledge over eternal access to God. So, despite having already been given dominion over the whole planet by their creator, the pair chose not to believe His dire warning. They opted instead to believe satan's[ii] suggestion that the forbidden fruit would make them like God. Thereby they chose their own intellects above the sovereignty of God, with the mistaken idea that only then would they be like Him. In one fell swoop, their choice lost them their close relationship with the Lord, brought death on all mankind and surrendered their dominion of the world to a human-hating fiend. The truth is that, because they were made in His image, Adam and Eve were already like God. All they had to do was to opt for Him.

While the history of mankind, especially as exhibited by the children of Israel, can be seen as the story of the human endeavour to get back to God, Ephesians 1:4-6 makes it clear that God had a solution from before the creation of the world; it was always His plan that Jesus would one day restore us to everything good that God has for us, when we choose Him. The cross has opened the door for whole generations to reconnect with God, enabling the mystery of us living in Him and Him in us, through the infilling of His Holy Spirit. This wonderful fulfilment of Emanuel, meaning 'God with us', empowers us to walk in beautiful, creative faith which is larger than earthly life. But we have to choose to receive and work with this gift.

To repent means to change your thinking. While born-again Christians host the presence of God, we have the daily choice of whether or not to hook up to the mind of Christ (1 Corinthians 2:16) or to give in to the old ruts of previous thinking. This manual is all about how we can choose to use our faith imagination to dialogue with the Lord, within a landscape of heavenly settings. As long as we are surrendered to Christ, imagining with Him can only bring revelation and many good fruits. Then we discover how beneficial it is to be able to immerse ourselves in the richness of what God has already planted within us, to discover the 'yes and amen' of God and choose LIFE.

When thinking works against God, it is never more clearly demonstrated than when we choose to think negatively: moaning, complaining, grumbling, criticism (of God, others and self), discouraging words (including gossip), pessimism and even careless talk, e.g."I'm *dying* to see you". When the people of Israel 'grumbled in their tents' (Deuteronomy 1:26-33), the Lord saw it for what it was; choosing not to trust Him. Where there is lack of trust in God, it is easy to be terrified by any storm that might whip up around us. Fear is the polar opposite of God's perfect love. Yet our Maker wants us to know that He will 'fight for [us]' (Deuteronomy 1:30), He calms the storm as told in Mark 4:35-41 and He has only good plans for us, to give us 'hope and a future' (Jeremiah 29:11). We can choose to say "Yes" to these facts, because 'in Him it has always been "Yes"' (2 Corinthians 1:19).

In 2 Corinthians 10:5, Paul is emphatic about choosing to take every thought captive. This is because negative thinking stops us co-labouring with God. When we take our eyes off God, we can get diverted by soulish thinking which centres around the self and essentially pushes God off the throne of our heart. Such distraction from God's good and perfect purposes plays into the enemy's plans to 'steal and kill and destroy' (John 10:10). Mark Virkler (cited in Arnott 2012) came to the startling realisation that all positives come from God and all negatives come from the enemy. God is good all the time; the exact opposite is true of satan[ii]. We have a choice to partner with God's goodness, rather than with the enemy.

We need to choose to be proactive in displacing negative thoughts, which have a habit of rattling around in our brains when left unattended. Indeed, "fasting" from negativity improves quality of life. Don Gossett's (1976) book, *What You Say Is What You Get*, is a helpful tool for nipping negatives in the bud. Changing our thinking and spoken words halts the far-reaching effects of destructive thought cycles and opens heavenly doors previously locked by the bolts of negativity. Many versions of Ephesians 4:23 speak about the human mind having a spirit. When we choose to surrender this spirit of our mind to God, then we can co-labour with him in a process of divine exchange. This is where we willingly boot out the bad thoughts and invite Holy Spirit to replace them with their direct opposites. This exercise ushers in God's righteousness and holiness. It may feel impossible to begin with, but we 'can do all this through Him who gives [us] strength' (Philippians 4:13) and it gets easier with practise.

Choosing not to connect our mind to the mind of Christ is to disconnect from the heavenly and trust only in the confines of our mortal experience. As Christians, we have chosen to be grafted into Jesus as 'The Vine' (John 15:5) and this automatically grafts us into the mind of Christ. When we engage our mind with His, we have the key to discerning how our Father God sees the universe and how we fit into it. Such interfacing enables us to see eternal things, which cannot be seen with ordinary human eyes. Then, anything good is possible. But we have to choose to work with Him in mind and spirit.

Imagination as a heavenly weapon:
Godly imagination is also a rather excellent weapon against our foe. In Zechariah 1:18-21, the prophet has a vision in which the creativity of the Lord's craftsmen scatters the 'horns' of the enemy, thereby breaking the power of enemy strategies. This is most mysterious, but I like the idea of Godly creativity messing up enemy strategies. And it is the creativity of our sanctified imagination that can help us to win the battle of the mind. The Passion Translation of Matthew 6:19-23 urges us to 'stockpile heavenly treasures' and speaks of the eyes of our spirit allowing revelation light to enter our being. When we allow our surrendered imaginations to build heavenly repositories and connect to Kingdom revelation, we develop a healthy respect for the sheer vastness and joy of what God has made attainable to us; as previously said, it is immeasurably more than we can ask or imagine by our own endeavours. Indeed, we find that the storehouses of Heaven are much bigger and more "real" than anything on Earth.

Imagination and inner healing:
The ministry of inner healing has long encouraged people to imagine themselves back in a painful situation, in order to ask Jesus into that place and heal the emotional/spiritual wound. This kind of healing is wonderfully miraculous, because it takes a past event, invites in the eternal to heal the historical fly in the ointment and brings life-improving changes for a person's present and future.

When my late husband, Graham, suddenly collapsed and died, my two grown-up daughters had troubling memories surrounding the traumatic events of that night; Jo, the elder, had recurring images of seeing Graham lying dead on the hospital "resus" trolley and Georgia, the younger, kept returning to images of him being resuscitated during transfer from our home to the ambulance. They agreed to let me pray with them, one at a time, and we asked Holy Spirit to come.

When I asked Jo what she could see in her mind's eyes, she told me she could see her dad lying dead on the "resus" couch in Accident and Emergency. I asked if anything else was happening, hoping that she would be able to see Jesus, but she was unable to progress. So, I shared with her my mental picture of Graham sitting up, swinging his legs to the side of the bed and saying, "Jo, come and tuck me in". I suggested she do this in her mind's eye. "What shall I say?" Words instantly flowed into my mind; "Say: 'Night night Daddy, see you in the morning.'" So this is what she did. The recurring images stopped and those touching words, full of tenderness and hope, have been inscribed on Graham's tombstone.

With the younger daughter, I told her of Joyce Huggett's (1996) experience in which God seemed to bring down a screen to protect her from seeing upsetting images. My daughter was able to bring the distressing scenario to mind and we then asked Holy Spirit to help her to stop seeing it. After a few minutes, and with some excitement, she said "A massive angel wing has appeared between me and Daddy's body... and it's golden!" This helped to reduce such traumatic memories for her. See Chapters 6 and 9 for more descriptions of how the imagination can be used for inner healing.

Imagination, when submitted to God, can bring beautiful relief from suffering. *The Garden* is an extension of this idea, utilising a heavenly space to encounter the power of God to see change for the better. We don't have to have had a painful situation in our lives in order to go to *The Garden*. Yet, amongst other things, it can be a place of healing.

Chapter 3

The Garden: A Meeting of Two Minds

'I slept but my heart was awake.'
(Song of Songs 5:2)

This chapter explores different ways in which the imagination is used in every day thought and how it can open doors to the heavenly. There are a number of activations to test and grow your faith imagination.

Concrete, abstract and creative thinking:
Distinguishing between concrete, abstract and creative thinking helps to ascertain where a person might be on the scale of imaginative ability. To begin with, concrete thinking is the capacity to interpret life using only the physical senses of the immediate surroundings, whereas abstract thinking is the capability to imagine what is not right in front of us. Most people begin life interpreting the world around them by utilising concrete thinking, simply through their five senses, until they increase their aptitude to imagine things that are not directly before them.

So we all use our imagination in varying degrees. The development of thinking abstractly is highly practical, enabling us to plan ahead rather than focussing only on the here and now, as well as to dream and form new ideas. Most of us dream, creating "videos" in our minds without any immediate stimuli, allowing many of us of think in the abstract. Even babies whimper or smile in their sleep, long before they have any concept of dreaming abstractly; they dream what babies dream and demonstrate a God-given ability to think beyond the concrete. Of course, people are very diverse; our age, varying natural abilities and life experiences will mean that everyone's interpretation of the world will differ. The next two activations, on page 26 and 27, are designed to help you further distinguish between concrete and abstract thinking.

Creative thinking is a step beyond the abstract and involves the utilisation of one's personal experiences, to develop a unique way of interacting with the world around us. So an artist may paint a garden, but add in "twists" from their imagination to create deeper meaning. They may even paint a garden entirely from their imagination. What's more is that Christian artists will blend their creative instincts with heavenly material,

Activation 1
Concrete thinking
Allow 5 minutes for this activation

Get yourself a drink and take it to a peaceful place, where you can sit comfortably.

Then actively appreciate everything about your drink.

Take notes on the following:

- *the colour, shape, weight and temperature of the cup/glass;*
- *how you lift and tip the cup/glass up to your mouth;*
- *the smell, taste and temperature of your drink;*
- *the sound you make when you sip and swallow.*

This is concrete thinking, in which you interpret exactly what your senses experience.

Activation 2
Abstract thinking

Allow 5-10 minutes for this activation

Find a peaceful place, where you won't be disturbed, and sit comfortably.

Write down the directions of how to get from your home to your closest shops, making sure every turn is included.

This is abstract thinking. You are able to do this by retrieving visual and other sensory memories, which remind you of those places along the way to the shops, making it possible for you to write down the directions without actually going there.

to produce Godly revelation. Below is a picture, by prophetic artist Linda Mellor, which resulted from a series of dreams. It represents God's plan for

Prophetic Picture for Healing Rooms Scotland, by Linda Mellor

Healing Rooms in Scotland. Who has ever seen a door on a Scottish hilltop, a giant shining tree or a sun made of jewels? Yet, the artist's creative expression brings deeper meaning to the idea of spiritual access into Scotland, future growth and God's favour. She has used familiar concrete images to create heavenly, abstract ideas, through artistic representation, in order to bring multi-layered, spiritual significance.

In this manner, when we allow our God-given minds to connect with the mind of Christ, we can apply creative thinking to Scripture and the knowledge of God. As previously mentioned, there has been a long tradition in the western church of divine reading or *lectio divina*. This is a practice of reading and meditating on Scripture as living Word, in order to deepen one's relationship with God, develop understanding of His Word and access deeper revelation of the mind of Christ. A simple technique of practising divine reading is to read a passage of Scripture and then spend time meditating on it, by imagining oneself either as one of the characters or as a bystander. In this fashion, it is possible to interact with the scenario and glean deeper insight. In a very simple way, this is essentially putting flesh on the bones of the text and making the written word more "real". You'll find a *lectio divina* activation near the end of this chapter, on page 36.

The art of visualisation:
People are generally more receptive to learning and remembering when they *see* what is being taught. It's the old adage of 'a picture speaks a thousand words'. Furthermore, it is now known that creating mental images not only helps learning but also helps to improve memory. While the act of forming an image does require focus and concentration, the images formed stick in the mind more easily than simply reading words on a page. So imagining *The Garden* will help a person learn with the Lord and better remember what He teaches (though it is always best to write down such experiences in a journal, to help remember and clarify them later).

Visualisation simply means seeing things in our mind's eye. It is used subconsciously by most people every day. When used consciously it is known to help us learn and remember. Gymnasts and dancers will close their eyes and use neuroplastic—brain changing—visualisation techniques, to run through their routines repeatedly in their heads. Without actually doing the physical programme, their minds and muscles "believe" that they've done the drill to a certain extent. Furthermore, repeated visualisation forges stronger neural pathways, which actually improve muscle memory as well as confidence, consistency and performance. As such, visualisation is less about fooling the brain and more about actual mind building and genuine experience. Visualisation of *The Garden* is like visualising the routine in the gym, but it helps us to build spiritual muscle memory, as well as spiritual senses; which all help to shape us up into being the people who God designed us to be. Our relationship with the Lord is not performance based, but when we start to visualise *The Garden,* we are able to reinforce our relationship with Him in a way that also fosters confidence and consistency.

Although we use our imagination to go there, it soon becomes clear that *The Garden* is not a fabrication of our own making; it is heavenly real estate, which belongs to God and He is the Lord of that place. It is when we surrender our imagination to Him and invite Jesus to come into *The Garden* of our hearts, that we realise that, in actual fact, He is inviting us into *His* garden. It is this shared space with the Lord where we can firmly establish our relationship with Him.

Overleaf is a *Litmus Test* activation to see if you can readily access your imagination. It involves your five senses in a task of remembering something evocative and yet relatively ordinary. If you manage to engage one or more of your senses in your imagination, you are ready for a first foray into *The Garden*.

Activation 3
Litmus test for your imagination, using your memory and five senses
Allow 5 minutes for this activation

Find a peaceful place, where you won't be disturbed, and sit comfortably. You are going to try to evoke a clear memory of your favourite food, without that food being anywhere near you, by activating your five senses in order to imagine the:

- o **Appearance** *of the food, including colour, size and shape;*
- o **Smell** *of the food—you know you're doing well if your salivary glands are activated as a result;*
- o **Feel** *of the food in your hands and mouth, noting texture as you imagine holding, chewing and swallowing it;*
- o **Taste** *of the food—again, salivary flow is a sure sign you're imagining well;*
- o **Sound** *made by the food as you eat it.*

- *Ask Holy Spirit to help you;*
- *Now close your eyes and picture your favourite food in your mind's eye, using all your senses.*

What to do if you've tried and failed to engage your imagination:
It is likely that everyone has the capacity to imagine in one way or another. However, it may be easier for some than for others. For those that simply can't imagine anything at all, there may be a mental, physical or spiritual obstruction preventing them from accessing the gift.

I once knew a man who had totally shut down his imagination, as a way to protect himself from sinning; a kind of "plucking out the mind's eye" to prevent his imagination from straying. So absolute was the problem that he was unable to picture a mere cucumber in his head. It was when he found he was incapable even of imagining his wife's face that he realised how complete and unwholesome his blanket banishment of his imagination had become. In his attempt to nip all unhelpful fantasy in the bud, he had inadvertently caused full blockage of his ability to visualise anything at all with his mind, including the good. With this newfound insight and some sensitive guidance from a Christian counsellor, he was able to develop a healthy approach to using his imagination. Godly thinking is like a tightrope walk, in which the centre of our balancing pole

The spiritual journey as a tightrope walk
(painting by the late Sarah McCrum)

carries truth and goodness, while the threats and negatives are kept at a distance. In this way, it is entirely possible, as well as desirable, to walk the fine line without losing the ability to fully appreciate healthy creativity.

God is speaking all the time:
If you are having a problem being able to imagine, simply ask God to tell you what the root of the problem is and ask Him to show you how to fix it. If you are not very used to God speaking to you, the book *Four Keys To Hearing God's Voice* by Mark Virkler (2013) is a good introduction. It is well worth knowing that God is speaking to you all the time; though not usually in an audible voice. I imagine His Words flowing like a river; all we have to do is step into that river and catch the words that are flowing past. Sometimes it's like tuning into a radio station, until the white noise disappears and we get clarity. God often speaks very quickly and because we have the mind of Christ, when in listening mode, we can work with whatever it is that pops into our heads. Listening is a process, so write down what you hear, think and see and follow it through. Do ask the Lord questions. He will answer, even if it's not in the way or the timescale that you might anticipate. Expect the unexpected.

Whether your imaginative difficulty is physical, mental or spiritual, ask God to show you how to access the healing Jesus bought for you on the cross. Remember that the original meaning of Isaiah 53:5 is that by His wounds we WERE healed, yesterday, today and forever; it is a finished work of the cross, once and for all, and He 'has done it!' (Psalm 22:31). We often unconsciously close doors to our own healing, but Holy Spirit is our instructor, teacher, counsellor and guardian and, if we are willing to co-labour with Him, He is eminently able to set us free. So keep exploring.

Perseverance is key:
Sometimes, people feel that imagining Heaven in their hearts is just too difficult. They may gain access one day, but not another and so lose heart. This can happen especially if self esteem is low or if fear and anxiety rob a person of their trust in the process. But, if this is a new skill for you, it will take time to develop. So be encouraged and keep practising. *The Garden* is a place where you will soon learn how precious you are to the Lord and how safe you are in His presence. 'There is now no condemnation for those who are in Christ' (Romans 8:1) and in *The Garden* He will bring you joy, humour and beauty, as well as answers to the obstacles you are trying to surmount.

Sometimes the Lord allows a blockage to arise in order to encourage us to deepen our search, to teach us patience or simply because His agenda happens to be different to ours. So keep persevering and be experimental, because 'it is the glory of God to conceal a matter; to search out a matter is the glory of kings' (Proverbs 25:2) and that means us, because we are royal children of The King of the Universe. Sometimes however, when you have been in *The Garden* many times, over a long period, and have caught up with where God wants you to be, it is just a matter of occasionally checking in to see if there has been any more movement in a particular area.

When your spiritual senses fail you, remember instead:
Bill Johnson (2018) says that when we feel unable to see, God asks us what we can hear and that when we feel unable to see or hear, God asks us to remember. A friend of ours was convinced that she would not be capable of imagining *The Garden*, even though she was easily able to complete the litmus test activation on page 30. So when it came down to imagining *The Garden*, she chose instead to remember earthly gardens she knew well. When reporting back, this lady told us about seeing all the flowers in her own garden at home, each bloom carrying meaning.

Significantly, she also remembered an incident involving the garden where she grew up. In this remembrance, she was about two years old and crawled into the family chicken coop to collect an egg. She knew that if she tried to climb out the same way she clambered in, she might drop and break the egg, so she just sat there waiting to be found for what seemed like hours, cupping the egg in her hands, until her frantic mother finally found her. She was helped to prayerfully invite Jesus back into this memory, in much the same way as in inner healing. Then she was able to follow Jesus out of the coop, through an exit He created, without breaking her egg. "What did you do with the egg?" I asked. "I gave it to my mum." "What did Jesus say to you", I enquired. "Good girl!" Being able to visualise *The Garden* is always a process and memory can be very helpful in engaging the Divine along the way.

The next activation is designed to help you kick start and develop your imaginative abilities:

> ## Activation 4
> ## *Kick starting your imagination:*
> *Allow 30-90 minutes for this activation*
>
> ### Part 1
>
> - *Ask Holy Spirit to help you;*
> - *Take your journal and pen to a local garden or park, ideally on a dry day and with something to eat or drink for the taste element;*
> - *Sit and take in your surroundings;*
> - *In your journal, write down what you:*
>   - **See**
>   - **Smell**
>   - **Feel**
>   - **Taste**
>   - **Hear**
>
> *Pay attention to every detail. You may need to shut your eyes to enable you to focus on senses other than sight.*
>
> ### Part 2
> *Allow about 10 minutes for this part of the activation*
>
> - *As soon as you get home, find a quiet place where you won't be disturbed and sit comfortably;*
> - *Read your journal notes about the garden/park you have just visited;*
> - *Ask Holy Spirit to help you;*
> - *Now close your eyes and, one by one, remember all the things you saw, smelt, felt, tasted and heard. Refer to your journal if you need to;*
> - *Repeat as often as required, to awaken and strengthen your abstract imagination. This should help to make "visible", in your mind's eye, that which is not immediately in front of your eyes;*
> - *When you feel confident, start asking Jesus where He is in the garden/park you visit. Write it down. Ask more questions and expect to get answers.*

A first foray into a biblical garden:
The activation overleaf is an exercise in *lectio divina*, asking God to help you meditate on the Garden of Eden in Genesis 2:8-17 and using your sanctified imagination to experience the scriptural elements in your mind's eye. You can use this method with almost any passage of the Bible, but this manual focuses on biblical gardens.

I recently asked the Lord to show me what the two trees were like in the centre of the Garden of Eden. I was amazed to see the Tree of life as an enormous evergreen, with no visible fruit. Once I got over my surprise, I worked out that to find the fruit you have to climb up inside the tree, with no obvious branches on the trunk. Proverbs 2 encourages us to search for the knowledge of God as if for silver. It's like a treasure hunt; God seems hidden, but He's not if you look for Him. He delights to see us find heavenly footholds to climb higher and higher into Him, to discover His heavenly treasures hidden aloft.

On the other hand, I saw the tree of the knowledge of good and evil as a short tree with many brightly coloured fruit, which are all relatively easy to reach. While it must have been hard for Adam and Eve to ignore such an attractive tree, it was the only tree of all the trees in the whole garden which God explicitly forbade them to eat the fruit of, because it would make them die if they did. All God wants is an obedient people, who hear His voice and follow Him where He leads and that's often via the less obvious route.

Activation 5
Lectio divina: the first garden
Allow about 20 minutes for this activation

- *Find a quiet place, where you won't be disturbed, and sit comfortably;*
- *Have your journal at the ready, to write down and capture your findings;*
- *Ask Holy Spirit to bless and anoint you as, you read about the Garden of Eden;*
- *Read Genesis 2:8-17;*
- *Now read the same passage again and write down all the elements that appear in this Scripture;*
- *Then surrender your sanctified imagination to the Lord, close your eyes and imagine all the elements of Eden in your mind's eye. Ask Jesus to show you around the Garden of Eden. Use as many senses as possible to connect yourself with this particular garden;*
- *Write down anything that strikes you in any way. Draw what you see, if you can. Feel free to break off at intervals along the way, to take notes/draw, and then simply take up where you left off.*

Ask yourself:

- What do the rivers and trees of Eden look like?
- Are there other things you have imagined that are not mentioned in the Bible reading?
- What are the colours of Eden?
- How does it make you feel?
- Where is Jesus in Eden?
- What is Jesus saying/doing?
- Have you learnt something new?

Write down any surprises from this experience.

Chapter 4

Exploring The Garden

"I have come home at last! This is my real country! I belong here. This is the land I have been looking for all my life, though I never knew it till now... Come further up, come further in!"
(Lewis, 2009)

This chapter is scattered with personal experiences of *The Garden,* which I like to call "walking in Scripture", to demonstrate the way in which the faith imagination of a believer can lead to deep, meaningful and life-changing encounters with the Word. On page 39 there is a *lectio divina* activation focussing on Revelation 4, to encourage you to take the heavenly territory that is your rightful inheritance as a child of God. Following that, there is an activation to facilitate your first foray into *The Garden* of your own heart.

If the last chapter's activation on the Garden of Eden was a new experience for you, then you have now discovered that Scripture is territory in which you have heavenly permission to wander. It's a step beyond remembering your own experience. When you imagined your route to the shops in the activation on page 27, you did so by accessing your memories of previous trips to the shops. When you imagine Scripture, especially those passages that lend themselves to *The Garden*, you are not only using your own pre-existing knowledge of life and the Word, but you are also accessing God's memories, thoughts, ideas, plans, feelings and presence. This is because *The Garden* really belongs to Him.

As already established in previous chapters, the experiential and immersive approach of *The Garden* brings more depth and dimensions to the meaning of the Word; with increased relevance to one's personal walk with the Lord, as well as accelerated learning and renewing of the mind. The faith imagination changes the two dimensions of reading a Bible story into a three-dimensional experience. What's more is that other dimensions become apparent in *The Garden*, because heavenly space is eternal space; there is always more with God and so there is always more in *The Garden*.

I first did an eight-minute meditation on Revelation 4, at a Jesus Ministry conference in 2012, as a citizen of Heaven. That short meditation was quite a revelation to me. I not only observed that Heaven is like a giant garden, with many *al fresco*—outdoor—features, but realised that Scripture could become as many-layered and multi-faceted as actual encounter, if not more so. Additionally, I discovered that when you give space to God, He fills it; things happen, in that heavenly place, which are not specifically written down in the Bible.

Is this kind of experience valid? Can we trust anything that isn't written in the Bible? Well, we know that many things Jesus did are not written down in the Bible (John 21:25). And there will always be more to God than we can "see at first sight"; He says 'Call to me and I will answer you and tell you great and unsearchable things you do not know' (Jeremiah 33:3). Besides, *The Garden* is very scriptural, as we have already discovered in previous chapters and many of the elements you will find there will resonate with biblical precedent. Moreover, *The Garden* fosters intimacy with the Lord, which is His great call to the church of Ephesus in Revelation 2:4. And the spirit of *The Garden* is one of encouragement, as well as deeper learning. So relax, have a go at the next activation and see what the Lord wants to show you in Revelation 4:

Activation 6
Being a citizen of Heaven in Revelation 4
Allow 10-20 minutes for this lectio divina activation

- *Find a quiet place, where you won't be disturbed, and sit comfortably;*
- *Have your journal at the ready, to write down and capture your findings;*
- *Ask Holy Spirit to bless and anoint you as you read Revelation 4;*
- *Now read the same passage again and write down all the elements that appear in this scripture;*
- *Then surrender your sanctified imagination to the Lord, close your eyes and imagine all the chapter elements in your mind's eye. Ask Jesus to show you around this heavenly place, using as many senses as possible to connect with God there;*
- *Write down anything that strikes you in any way. Draw what you see if you can. Feel free to break off at intervals along the way, to take notes/draw, and then simply take up where you left off.*
    - *Are there things you have imagined that are not mentioned in the Bible?*
    - *What colours can you see?*
    - *How does it make you feel?*
    - *Where is Jesus? What is He saying/doing?*
    - *Where is Father God?*
    - *Have you discovered new insights?*

When I did this Revelation 4 activation for the first time, I saw Jesus beckoning me up a cloud staircase to a door which opened onto a grassy hillside. Far away in a deep and wide valley, the Father was waving to us while sitting on His throne on top of a mountain in the middle of the basin below. Now, Revelation 4 does not mention a mountain, but there it was in my meditation. It just goes to show that when we enter God's territory on His terms, He will show us the bigger picture. And there is indeed a mountain in Heaven; as Hebrews 12:22 states, 'you have come to Mount Zion and to the city of the living God, the heavenly Jerusalem'. I was truly grateful that I did not have to tremble with fear, like the Israelites did at the bottom of Mount Sinai, but could approach the living God as a child running to my Daddy. Even now, I am quite touched by this tender and excited greeting by my Maker.

My sketch of Revelation 4

Behind Him fireworks exploded, lightning flashed and the emerald rainbow glowed. Thunder rumbled and I could hear the fireworks crackle and bang in my "mind's ear". I rolled joyfully down the grassy hill and Jesus explained that every blade of grass I touched represented a person I came into contact with on Earth, which made me feel overawed and concerned about missed opportunities. At the bottom of the hill, the Sea of Glass stretched out in front of the mountain. I was delighted to hear the waves tinkling as they crashed on the shore and to discover that this sound was produced by a myriad of diamonds in the surf. And that was that. Our eight-minute meditation was up.

A month later, I spent much more time in Revelation 4. I am not a very good artist, but drawing helps to consolidate the experience and bring all the elements together into one picture (see opposite page). I included the cloud steps and fireworks from my encounter the previous month, building on past experience. A ruby/jasper Father God waves happily in the centre, with a representation of an emerald rainbow and lightning behind Him. Seven lamp stands sit in front of Him and twelve of the twenty-four elders can be seen sitting on thrones below Him—the other twelve are on the other side of the mountain—lifting their crowns in readiness to lay before the Father. At that stage I hadn't yet drawn the four living creatures; these came later on, after repeated excursions to Revelation 4. Later, the foundations of Heaven in Revelation chapter 20 were (and still are) to become of great fascination for me.

I view walking in Revelation 4 as us walking in the garden of God's heart and *The Garden* as walking with God in the garden of our own heart; the garden which has been growing and maturing ever since we first came to know Jesus as our Saviour, whether we are aware of it or not. Having done the Revelation 4 activation, it's now time for you to see what your own heavenly garden is like. Don't worry about vagueness when you see things in your mind's eye. God's thinking is in the inkling, so simply go with the flow, grab whatever impressions you get and follow them through. The door to *The Garden* of your own heart is open. Enter in by doing the activation over the page.

Activation 7
The ten-minute garden
Entering The Garden of your own heart
Allow about 10 minutes for this activation

- *Find a quiet place, where you won't be disturbed, and sit comfortably;*
- *Have a pen ready to write down your impressions;*
- *Ask Holy Spirit to bless and anoint you;*
- *Close your eyes and imagine your heart as a garden;*
- *Ask Jesus to take you by the hand and show you around your garden;*
- *What are you and Jesus doing in your garden?*
- *Ask Jesus questions about your garden and take note of His replies;*
- *Don't rush. Take your time;*
- *Record what you see, using all your senses. It's all right to open your eyes periodically to write/draw your findings and then go back to The Garden, to pick up where you left off.*

There is infinite room for development here, so it's a good idea to return to your ten-minute garden each day, or as frequently as you are able, to discover more. Jesus is the Lord of Time and He will just pick up where you left off.

I see many pictures in my mind's eye. It wasn't always this way. It first happened in my late twenties, when I sought to deepen my relationship with the Lord. As a young mum, I hadn't been having quiet times and felt like a mediocre Christian. So I determined that I would start giving time to the Lord every day, during my toddler's afternoon nap. The first appointed day arrived, my small daughter was asleep and I looked for my Bible. I couldn't find it anywhere. I got a bit stroppy and said to God "If You want me to have a quiet time with You, You're going to have to find my Bible!" Instantly a picture of my Bible appeared in my head; it was on the floor behind the bathroom door. "I've looked there already!" I replied, exasperated. Silence ensued, with a sense of God smiling wryly. Obediently, and with some trepidation, I crept down the hall and peered behind the bathroom door. And there it was; my Bible was leaning up against the back of the door, just as the picture had indicated. Since then, the pictures haven't stopped coming. In fact, they are so many that I once asked God if He could please just talk to me like normal people. The answer was "No!" It's a gift He's given me and it's to be developed.

The first time I ever visited what I came to know as *The Garden* of my own heart, I was not actually looking for it. I knew about Revelation 4, but I didn't really know that I had a heavenly garden inside of me. I was fifty-two, widowed and dating Ray. Grief and new-found love both created opportunities for God to communicate with me on a deeper level. I was seeking greater intimacy with Jesus at the time and, in my mind's eye one afternoon, He stood before me with a double-edged sword sticking out of His mouth. While I took the words of Song of Songs 1:1 very seriously— 'Let Him kiss me with the kisses of His mouth'—I couldn't envisage how I could bypass that large sword obstructing the space between our respective lips. But there He stood, seeming to say, "Just try anyway". So I did. In my imagination, I felt the only way to kiss Jesus was to swallow the sword first, but a very strange thing happened; I not only swallowed the sword, but Jesus too! Then, in my mind's eye, I was aware that Jesus was very much *in* me, crashing about in my garden and cutting down hedges. "What are you doing!" I cried, appalled. "Just weeding," He replied. It makes me laugh to think of it now.

And so began quite a long journey of healing in my garden, which I visited frequently, for ten minutes or so in my early morning quiet times before work. In my mind's eye, I began in a compost heap. I can only imagine that this signified my lack of self worth in comparison to God's true view of me, despite being active at church and a confident and responsible leader in the NHS.

Then, one morning, the compost heap was gone and I found myself standing in a plunge pool directly beneath a waterfall, surrounded by tall, thick hedges. It felt very private and safe. I washed under this waterfall for what seemed like months of quiet times. Sometimes rainbows would dance in the spray, signifying promise and hope. Eventually, a time came when a door frame appeared in the plunge pool and I had a season of seemingly transitioning from one side of the frame to the other. I can't say entirely what process was going on here, but I just went with the flow and accepted it; like a child being cared for by a loving parent. The symbolism is clearly about cleansing, but it was more than washing me clean; there was also healing and development of confidence in God's love for me. The truth of the cross is more than just an idea and it is more than just a fact; it is a multidimensional, mysterious, but loving reality that touches all of our body, soul and spirit. And I was being changed by this ever patient, gentle force of Heaven in the safety of my garden.

As an aside, when I think back, it reminds me of the time I first asked Jesus to dress me in the armour of God (see Ephesians 6:10-18). I'd been taught to dress myself daily in this armour thirty years before, after experiencing some unpleasant paranormal activity. However, it's a different ballgame when Jesus puts on your armour; it doesn't fall off for one thing. Each piece develops a depth of meaning that couldn't be seen before. Since then, I've discovered more pieces of biblical armoury: a cloak of humility, a shofar of prophecy, a bow of discernment and arrows of faith, hope and love, rods of union and favour and I'm sure our heavenly toolbox has many more items for us to discover and utilise.

Back in *The Garden*, a day came when Jesus cut a hole in the hedge that surrounded the waterfall. This felt almost like an act of vandalism! I expressed my horror, but Jesus simply said "Come and look!" When I poked my head through the hole, I could see green and gently rolling hills sweeping away into the distance. Somehow, the waterfall had made me ready to expand my experience of *The Garden* and thus of God. Jesus called and a beautiful white horse cantered up to the hole in the hedge. It reminded me of Jesus' horse in Revelation 19:11. Jesus helped me up onto the horse and anointed my head with oil, such that it flowed onto the horse's back; a symbol of unity between us. The horse's name is Geyser, because he can shoot straight up like a fountain. But Geyser goes further than the stratosphere and into space, despite having no wings. I wonder if he represents Holy Spirit. When I ride him, I never fear nor fall off because I am one with him and, as I re-read this, my heart burns within me.

I found other features in *The Garden*, when I explored further. There is a beach where Jesus and I make sandcastles together. Play is very important in *The Garden*. We are repeatedly asked to come like little children by Jesus and children love to play. Development in Christ is an educational and family-building program, which is designed to be joy-filled. I also have a small formal garden with a fountain at its centre, where I can sit quietly enjoying the repeated patterns made by the plants and paths. Jesus and I have had many picnics under the trees, sitting on the grass. There, He has played with me as though I was a little child and He my father, or wrestled and teased me like a lover.

Once, He took me to a large shed in a small wood. I didn't want to enter the shed, because there was something ominous about it. Jesus spoke and the shed disappeared. I don't know what it represented exactly, but that didn't seem to matter. The most important thing was knowing that where Jesus is, there is no fear and no shame.

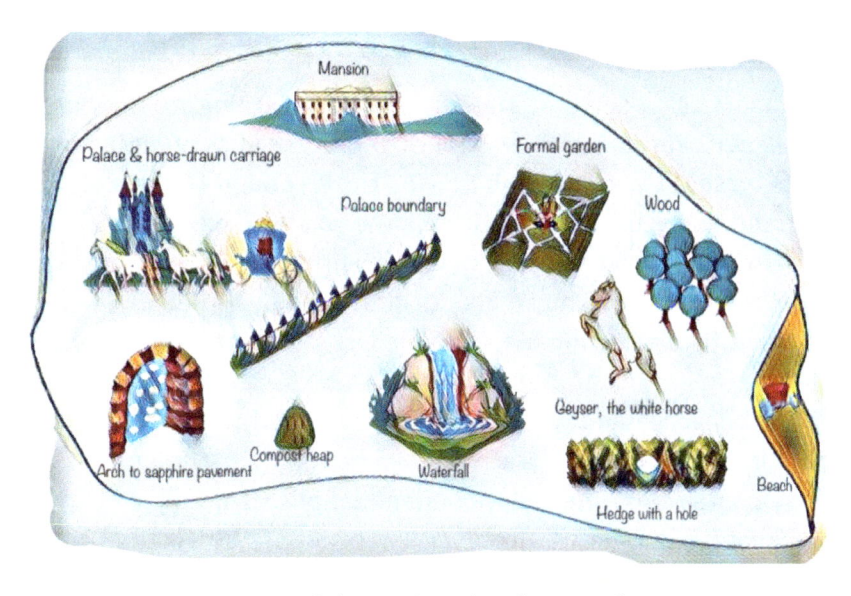

A map of The Garden of my heart so far

In my garden, I have a large white mansion set further uphill. It waits for me and isn't for now, I think. There is a palace surrounded by a hedged fence, behind which is a white, horse-drawn carriage. I can only assume that this represents my marriage to Ray, because so many Christians had prayer pictures of carriages drawn by four white horses in the months shortly before and after our wedding. Recently I found an arch, with access to the sapphire/lapis lazuli pavement of Exodus 24:10; to me this floor looks like cubic tiles of blue sky and white clouds. I am just beginning to find out what this means for me.

The map of *The Garden* of my heart, on the previous page, doesn't show the sea of glass. However, I have spent many a time beside the crystal sea, lying on a beautifully-crafted, open-curtained, four-poster bed. Funnily enough I've met others who also have a four-poster in their spiritual garden. Often I just lie down and gaze into Jesus' face. The bedspread is black, like the tents of Kedar in Song of Songs 1:5, and embroidered with gold to represent my life story. Bowls of fruit may appear on stands and different-coloured evening gowns might hang in midair, each colour signifying development in the Lord, waiting for me to try them on. Once, a chest of drawers appeared containing a wedding trousseau. Sometimes I skate on the surface of the sea, while at other times I swim beneath the ocean, where I am able to breathe underwater. There are times when I ascend the mountain to sit on Father God's lap. Sometimes He has things to say, but generally *The Garden* is much more about just *being* in God's presence.

It is important to say that when I first started going to *The Garden* to spend time with Jesus, satan[ii] was there, represented as an indistinct dark figure. He wasn't nearby, though he was close enough for us to hear him shouting shocking abuse at us. Although it was disconcerting, it was not sufficient for me to stop enjoying the Lord's presence. Indeed, my focus on Jesus drowned out the enraged insults of the enemy. Gradually, with time, the shadowy figure got further and further away until, one day, he just wasn't there anymore and he's never returned. As mentioned on page 13, we all carry baggage and satan's[ii] presence seemed to indicate that I had carried mine into my garden. It's possible that my battle against an old swearing habit at the time was the offending baggage. Whatever it was, I do know that being in Jesus' presence sorted it out. We don't always have to know the details of a healing, just that the goodness of the Lord is always supreme. Getting closer to His goodness brings good things. Intimacy with God drives out insult and accusation, just as God's perfect love drives out fear.

One time in *The Garden*, I took a journey on a boat, floating down a river, and I had to respond to a surprising turn of events. My boat veered onto the Sea of Galilee, which suddenly became very stormy. Jesus stood on the water some way away. I knew my challenge was to get out of the boat, like Peter, and get myself to Jesus. When I had previously read Matthew 14:22-33, I had not factored in that it was dark, that the wind was terribly strong and the waves horribly large, but this experience made all these elements very apparent and extremely demanding. It seemed an enormous effort to battle through the dark, wind and waves to get to Jesus, albeit in my mind's eye. He offered me no obvious help, but stood with His hand out, waiting. I got there in the end and, in that experience, I learnt always to focus on Him no matter how big the apparent obstacles.

That day, as part of my daily quiet time, I also learned about "journey will" and "end-point will", because I asked Jesus about what Colossians 1:9 meant about the church wanting to know His will. I thought that was obvious; surely that is The Great Commission of Matthew 28:18-20 and the second coming. "That's end-point will. We're talking about journey will," Jesus seemed to say, all sensed through impressions. He went on to explain that journey will is given only a bit at a time and cannot be foretold, but is co-created with Christ one step at a time. We never know how we'll respond to the challenges the Lord sets before us, but the aim is always to move on and not get stuck. As Christine Wren James (2012) writes, 'There are no exams, but whenever you sit God's test and you fail, you simply sit it again until you pass.' It's just that the test may look different the next time, to keep you on your toes.

There are many other deep experiences with God in my faith imagination, that have shaped me; though not always in *The Garden*. Once you allow Jesus to be the guide, like the incident with the armour of God, you enable the process of being taught by the Lord; in His time and in His way. I do know that when you are prepared to ask questions of Jesus, you need to be ready to listen carefully and write down His replies, because what He says can blow your socks off.

Such explorations of *The Garden* enable a process that is a kind of enlarging 'the place of your tent' (Isaiah 54:2), otherwise known as your heart. Once we realise that it's a never-ending process, we can relax and enjoy the journey of continual spiritual growth and know that nothing is wasted along the way. See Chapter 7, on page 73, for more about the ever expanding garden.

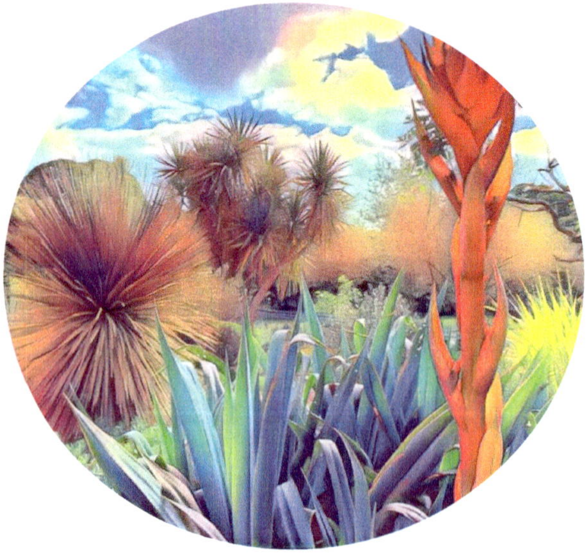

Chapter 5

Intimacy and *The Garden*

'I have come into my garden, my sister, my bride; I have gathered my myrrh with my spice. I have eaten my honeycomb and my honey; I have drunk my wine and my milk.'
(Song of Songs 5:1)

Song of Songs - a journey into intimacy and maturity:
Song of Songs, that short and mysterious book sitting near the centre of the Bible, is full of garden imagery that can be related to the journey we make into *The Garden* of our heart. On a very basic level, Song of Songs is King Solomon's story of a bride and a bridegroom longing for one another, presumed to be autobiographical. If taken at face value, it can feel almost too private to be of personal relevance.

However, if you think this is just about sex, you'll miss the dimensions of spiritual intimacy and relational development that are intrinsic to the flow of the chapters. Isaiah 54:5-6 declares to Israel, 'Your Maker is your husband'; God is Bridegroom and Israel the Bride. However, Psalm 22:27-28 and Joel 2:28 make it clear that all people (men included) are embraced in this relationship. It's not surprising then that Song of Songs is known as "the song of all songs"; the story of the divine romance between God and His people. Mark Davidson (2010) and Watchman Nee (1995), in their books *Becoming The Beloved* and *The Songs of Songs* respectively, explore how this short Bible volume symbolises God's pre-existing love for His Church and what can happen when the Church thinks like a Bride and learns to love God back.

Because Scripture is territory for us to inhabit, the way to understand the symbolism of Song of Songs is to immerse ourselves in it and read the book with the clear revelation that Jesus is the Groom and we are the

Bride, no matter what our gender. We often say, in the prophetic, that what is happening in Heaven has a natural counterpart on Earth. Ephesians 5:25 describes marriage as an echo of Christ's love for His Bride, the Church. In the beginning, Eve was taken from Adam's body and, by way of divine mystery, marital intercourse re-made them 'one flesh' (Genesis 2:24). This resonates with 1 Corinthians 6:17; the divine mystery of God becoming one with His people, through them being filled with His Holy Spirit. However, where earthly consummation requires bodily intercourse, with God it's Spirit to spirit; deep calls to deep (Psalm 42:7). So, when you make a concerted effort to exchange the sexual references in Song of Songs for spiritual encounter, you will have a much more enriching experience of a book that is like God's beating heart for His people.

Activation 8, over the page, is designed to be relished slowly and meticulously. When we get to know Song of Songs as a whole entity, we begin to see not only where we have been on our own Christian journey but where we are heading. When we dwell in the gardens of Song of Songs, we expand our spiritual boundaries and become empowered to run alongside Jesus.

You will find a key to the elements of Song of Songs on page 125. There are also chapter summaries of Song of Songs, on the pages following Activation 8, which you may prefer to read after you have completed it; that way, your experience will be founded on being led by the Lord rather than another person's interpretation. But, it does help to see Song of Songs as our journey of the Christian life; the process of falling in love with the Lord. The Groom's love is never failing and always encouraging. The Bride, however, finds that her passion waxes and wanes in the early chapters, until she discovers Her Lord is within *The Garden* of her heart and that she is called to co-labour with Him; giving Him everything she has in order to access "the more".

As you read Song of Songs, you will notice that The Groom's perspective is one of omnipresence and omniscience; always present and all knowing, just like God. The Bride's knowledge is much more reflective of our own limited perspective as human beings, yet the journey she travels promises heavenly growth inside and out.

Don't worry that some translations of Song of Songs alter who speaks in certain places, thereby changing the meaning. Such confusion might beg the question "Who is who?" However, because we are in God and He is in us, this paradox will always bring deeper implications and we can relax into the mystery instead of allowing confusion to halt our progress.

Activation 8
Immersive activation in becoming the Bride

This is a lectio divina activation, designed to be undertaken as a leisurely Bible study over a period of weeks. Your task is to imagine yourself as the Bride (even if you are male) and Jesus as the Groom, trusting that God is saying something directly to you through Song of Songs:

- *Find a quiet place, to sit comfortably, where you won't be disturbed;*
- *Find Song of Songs in your Bible. You may find it helpful to compare a couple of translations, e.g. NIV and The Passion Translation;*
- *Have your journal to hand;*
- *Ask Holy Spirit to guide and teach you, as you immerse yourself in Song of Songs. Feel free to use a Bible Commentary, but first listen to Holy Spirit and let yourself be taught by the Lord. There is a key to the meaning of many elements in Song of Songs on page 125;*
- *Read one chapter at a time (or take it more slowly and just concentrate on a few verses at a time);*
- *Re-read and write down things that jump out at you (see below);*
- *Close your eyes and imagine yourself as the Bride, in the section you are reading;*
- *Note down anything that feels significant to you;*
- *Take your time. This is not an activation to be rushed or undertaken lightly;*

- *Look out for spiritual imagery regarding:*

    - *Food*
    - *Animals*
    - *Furniture*
    - *Plants*
    - *Transport*
    - *Water*
    - *Precious stones/metals*
    - *Beds*
    - *Built structures*
    - *Drink*
    - *People*
    - *Countryside*
    - *Jewellery*
    - *Desert*
    - *Parts of the body*
    - *Cities*
    - *Rooms*
    - *Gardens*

Write down each element in your journal as you go; meditating on its meaning within the framework of the text as well as what it means to you.

A brief overview of Song of Songs, with a New Testament perspective

Chapter One:
The Bride aches for her lover, longs for His perfumed kiss and yearns for His chamber. Thankfully, her friends, the daughters of Jerusalem, champion her journey. Such encouragement is much needed, because the Bride not only feels her limitations but is bullied by her pharisaic brothers into caring for their vineyards; causing her to neglect her own. While the vineyard can be symbolic of Israel in the Bible, here it carries deeper meaning and can be taken to refer to the heart and God's Kingdom there. Meanwhile, the brothers' vineyard appears to represent faith that demands servitude rather than intimacy and passion.

Despite opposition, the Bride's aim is to find the one whom she loves. She is advised to venture out into the countryside, which always represents the territory of spiritual growth in Song of Songs and this "leave-to-seek" theme is repeated throughout the book. The Bride is nudged to get advice from the shepherds, who live and work in that pastoral environment and who might act as guides on the same journey to finding the Good Shepherd. At this early stage, the advice to go out and search is pondered but not yet fostered by the Bride. Such a quest feels immodest to her and her focus remains on the short cut to the Bridegroom's bed chamber, without the intervening search to find the Groom. The Bride is passionate, but not yet ready to step out of her comfort zone.

Then, for the first time, the Groom's voice interjects. Even at this early stage the lover of her soul appreciates the Bride's beauty, despite her foibles and struggles trapping her like one of Pharaoh's chariot horses; a representation of her old self stuck in a kind of soulish slavery. Essentially, Jesus is saying that He loves us right where we are now, no matter what our circumstances, and will enhance our beauty with jewellery of gold and silver; elements that represent purity and redemption. The lovers enjoy a feast, in which the release of the Bride's spikenard perfume portrays spiritual awakening, rising almost like incense. Feasting with the King is always about heavenly revelation. The Groom's fragrances of myrrh and henna blossom, signifying God's Royal garden, vineyard and very heart, seem to literally knock on the Bride's heart; dangling in a sachet over her chest. The lovers' first bed is *al fresco*, in the forest. For countryside read heavenly; forays into nature, in Song of Songs, are all about spiritual exploration into the divine.

Chapter Two:
Here we see the Bride and Groom not only in the countryside, but represented as plants in a beautiful, valley orchard. The Bride is the Rose of Sharon, like a lily among thorns, which resonates with Jesus' parable of the seed falling among thorns; the worries of life and the deceitfulness of wealth threatening to choke spiritual growth and prevent fruitfulness (Matthew 13:22) Nevertheless, the Bride has her eyes fixed on her Lord, who is like an apple tree. Here she finds rest beneath His branches, as well as sustenance in His fruit. Their love is again like a feast, in which apples from the King's orchard and raisins from His vineyard are strong metaphors for God's spiritual food, the bread of life, needed for growth of the human heart, indeed, the Bride is so hungry that she feels weak for the want of enough provision.

The Bride's resolve ebbs and flows at this stage; at one moment she is in the Groom's arms and the next she is all by herself in her bed. She sleeps and such sleep is evocative of spiritual torpor. The Groom seems ever to be calling her to awaken; a strong message to today's Church. The Bride senses the Groom approaching, like a gazelle leaping over the mountains and hills, which represent heavenly territory awaiting discovery. The Groom is half hidden by the lattice outside the Bride's window, which reminds us of our sketchy knowledge of our Lord, for we see only 'in part' (1 Corinthians 13:12) this side of Heaven.

The Bridegroom encourages His Bride to move beyond her wintry past, rise up and go with Him; the time is right and the season of growth has arrived. Moving from the confines of a comfy bed in order to run with the Lord, is a repeated "leave-to-cleave" theme. He sees that His Bride is stuck, as a dove hiding in the clefts of the rock, and exhorts her to look at Him and sing. If she will only catch the little foxes of the old, false self then she will be able to stop the damage they do in the beloveds' vineyard; the shared space of her heart with His.

While she loves to watch the way the Groom moves so freely, she is not yet ready to wake up and leave her indoor bed (here a symbol for "soulishness" and the old self). The gazelle-like Groom, browsing among the lilies of her heart, is a recurring image; He is always in *The Garden* of our heart, enjoying our spiritual journey there, even if we don't know it.

Chapter Three:
Chapter three sees the Bride bizarrely searching for the Groom from her indoor bed in the city. However, progress has been made from the sleepy Bride of chapter two; her unsettled state denotes a growing hunger for her Lord. Whereas the earthly marriage bed is for sleep and conjugal relations, Song of Songs makes it clear that there's much, much more in a relationship with God. Mark Marx, of Healing on the Streets, frequently says in his training 'Jesus is always on the move' and we need to keep up.

The city represents the Bride's earthly home; it is the place of her birth and guarded by watchmen appointed by men. As such, the city may be symbolic of the established church or even the old self. Cities are manmade and God is always calling to His Bride to escape such synthetic confines for the call of the wild, in which the countryside represents growing spiritual freedom. The great thing in this chapter is that the Bride does make a breakthrough. She leaves her bed and goes out to search the city, asking for help from the watchmen elders. So far, friends, shepherds and watchmen have all been willing to aid her in her quest to find the lover of her soul. We all need such help on our spiritual journey.

She finds her lover and they retire to the place where the Bride was first conceived, with nods to Psalm 139, in which we are reminded that she was knit together in her mother's womb by an all-seeing God. With such progress having been made, the lavish wedding parade simultaneously begins to advance from the dry places of the desert, reminiscent of the Israelites departing the desert for the Promised Land and strongly suggestive of the development of the Bride's heart. The desert is a repeated theme in Song of Songs. It seems to signify the journey of dying to self; leaving the dry desert of self for God's land of plenty. Indeed, the royal elements of the approaching matrimonial carriage seem to represent not only the coming and rightful position of her Lord's throne in her heart, but the Bride's elevation to royal status. This reminds us that the Church is not only the Bride of Christ, but is also seated 'with Him in the heavenly realms' (Ephesians 2:6).

Chapter Four:
Chapter four depicts the Groom's adoration of some of the Bride's physical attributes, from head down to breast. Such a partial inventory indicates that she has not yet given herself fully to the Groom. Remember to see this as spiritual surrender rather than sexual. While He is always full of love, the Groom longs for the Bride to come down from the "high places", that

denote the worship of other gods in the Old Testament and anything else 'that sets itself up against the knowledge of God' (2 Corinthians 10:5). She has not known that she has always had a garden in her heart; it is the Groom who now makes her aware of it. He reveals her garden as one which is walled, where the Groom describes His Bride as locked up, enclosed and sealed; mirroring her trapped nature from chapters one and two.

Despite the blockages, the Groom also depicts the Bride's true nature, the one chosen in Christ before the creation of the world, as a garden fountain and a well of flowing water. Always encouraging, the Groom tells of the richness of this garden; full of hidden treasure: orchards, incense and fragrant flowers. The Bride has already feasted a number of times with the Bridegroom, but something quite different happens in this chapter. Milk and honey, representing God's Word (as in 1 Peter 2:2 and Psalm 119:103), already flow in the Bride's mouth; she is no longer faint from hunger, but is now well fed and dripping with The Word. And milk and honey are not only advances on the apples and raisins of chapter two, but they are also reminders of the pledged attributes of the Promised Land (as told in Exodus 3:8). The Bride is coming into her spiritual inheritance.

And while her perfume has previously been spread in the presence of her King, now she is ready for even greater release. The Groom's myrrh, that knocked on the outside of her breast in that first chapter, is now inside *The Garden* of her own heart; mixed with her own spikenard and so much more. And it's all been waiting for such a time as this. Indeed, such enclosure has concentrated the fragrances of this walled garden. Nothing has been wasted, all of this time. The release will be intense. The blocked fountain has turned into the well of flowing water, representing a new ability for her heart to enlarge beyond its confines.

This is about the Bride stepping out in faith and sharing the beauty that has come from such intimacy with her Lord. When she asks the cold, bitter north wind and the warm, comforting south wind to blow on her garden, she is expressing a new revelation of her ability to spread her fragrance abroad to others, no matter what her circumstances. She knows that everything, from this time forth, will go into the pot and God will work good in it all (as asserted in Romans 8:28). A new and beautiful freedom has been discovered and a new depth of relationship forged.

Chapter Five:
Chapter five marks a very clear progression, in which the walled garden experience is over and it's time to move on again. It seems that every advance leads to a fresh challenge. Again we find the Bride asleep in bed, while the Groom is locked outside, knocking on the door to be let in. The journey of intimacy continues to be one of repeated awakenings.

And the Bride does awake; indeed her heart was awake throughout. However, because she *feels* unready yet again, as in Chapters one and two, the Bride is sluggish to respond and the Groom has gone by the time she opens the door. The city is not as helpful as in Chapter three and the Bride is beaten and robbed by the very watchmen designated to protect her. There is a resonance here with the response of the Pharisees to Jesus and to what we sometimes see in the Church today, when unadventurous elders feel threatened by the actions and intentions of those actively seeking God's eternal "more". The result is often to "shoot their own", allowing offence to translate into rejection and accusation. We can all be susceptible to such responses and need to let the Lord weed them out of our own gardens.

Yet, because God works good in all things, this attack causes the Bride to seek help from those who have always supported her. Such oneness in the belief and pursuit of God's love is highly reminiscent of Psalm 133's description of unity, as precious oil from Heaven. The friends prompt the Bride to remember what it is about the Groom that is better than anything else. In other words, when your spiritual senses fail you, remember instead. The Bride's response is to give a worshipful head-to-toe description of her beloved; our God, who is 'altogether lovely' (Song of Songs 5:16). When the going gets tough, it's always good to remember who God really is and what He has done in our lives so far. Significantly, the Bride's account of the Groom is the first full top-to-toe veneration to occur in Song of Songs; a sign of just how completely Jesus has given Himself to His Beloved.

Chapter Six:
In chapter six, the friends ask where the Groom has gone and the Bride has a light-bulb moment; she realises that He is in her garden! He is in her heart! God is within her! This inspires the Groom to do another head-to-breast veneration of His Bride, in which there is not one mention of her being trapped, blocked or sleepy. Rather, there He is in *The Garden* looking

to see if the vines and pomegranates are budding. Fruit is promisingly on the way.

At this very point, something wonderful happens; the Groom's desire for His Bride transports Him to the royal chariots of His people; resonant with the wedding carriage of chapter three. It is as if the desire of the Bride has whisked the Groom not only to her own side but to the very heart of all people, in a great wedding procession. This is the great call of the Bride to the Groom to 'come' in Revelation 22:20. The Bride is beginning to realise the power and authority she has in Christ.

Chapter Seven:
Chapter seven turns everything upside down. The Groom, for the first time, does not partially observe the Bride from top down; rather, He now has access to His whole Bride and starts to adore her from toe to top. This reversal is not by accident. Feet represent the Bride's willingness to finally follow the Groom wherever He goes and the Groom's full appreciation of His Bride is clearly representative of deepening and satisfying intimacy for both of them. The Bride's spiritual fruit are ripe, her cup is always full, everything about her is ready and all she wants is for all of it to go to her Lord. There is a complete surrender to God here, that hasn't existed previously.

With her newly-discovered authority in Christ, it is the Bride who sets the pace and now encourages the Groom to go with her to the countryside and villages, away from the manmade city of the old self and former ways of thinking. Together the Bride and Groom will check the buds on the vines and the pomegranate blossoms. It is as if this newfound drive is apostolic in nature, with a sense of nurturing *The Gardens* of other people's hearts. It is at this point that the Bride reiterates her desire to give the Groom everything; her whole being, the new as well as the old, the good as well as the bad. Nothing is wasted by God; He exchanges old, painful experiences for the fullness and bounty of Life in Him.

Chapter Eight:
Finally, chapter eight describes a "now-but-not-yet" longing, in which the Bride yearns for full unity with the Groom; to see Him face to face. She sees clearly how she was chosen, conceived and born under an apple tree, in a garden that is highly reminiscent of the Garden of Eden. She pledges her heart to God, knowing that He wears it like a seal on His arm; nothing can remove her from His love. She has absolute certainty that love is stronger

than death, fire or flood. God's love is like a mighty flame. It doesn't burn us up, because we have the fire of the Holy Spirit within us and fire does not burn fire.

The Bride's friends present her to the King, wondering if this little sister is yet a wall made for strong watchtowers or a door that should remain privately shut for now. But the Bride already knows her calling. She declares that she is a resilient wall and her breasts are already strong towers, for spiritual feeding and apostolic mothering of those around her, in order to bring contentment to her Lord.

She has clear certainty that she has come into her inheritance. While others only rent the King's vineyards, she does something completely different; not only does she freely *give* her vineyard (her heart) fully to Him, but she is prepared to pay the price for its upkeep. The last verse calls for those who dwell in the gardens, with friends in attendance, to let the Groom hear their voice; a call to us all to search for Him in *The Garden* of our hearts and dwell in *The Garden* of His heart.

Activation 9
Drawing parallels between your own life and that of the Bride in Song of Songs

Allow 10-20 minutes for this activation

- *Find a quiet place, where you won't be disturbed, and sit comfortably;*
- *Ask Holy Spirit to lead and guide you.*
- *Think about your Christian life so far.*
- *In what ways does your experience mirror the ebb and flow of the Bride's journey into God?*
- *Write down where you think you are in your bridal journey so far?*

***The Garden* of your spouse's heart:**
If you are married, you are one flesh and you may be able to take a peek into *The Garden* of your spouse's heart, to see what your union looks like there. Ten years ago, I was prayerfully wondering what *The Garden* of Ray's heart might look like. Immediately, I had an impression of a vast orchard, which spoke of the fruitfulness of Ray's heart. I asked the Lord, "Where am I in this orchard?" In response, little blue fairy lights appeared to be strung on the trees, giving a sense of beautification, celebration and fun; perhaps even of a multitude of tiny fruits of light. In the centre of this orchard was an enormous lighthouse, with one beam shining straight out over us. We climbed the lighthouse, which then transformed into Jesus; as tall as a giant. He then proceeded to stride out into the middle of Norfolk, with us perched on His shoulders. Pictures speak a thousand words and, in a very short time, God had shown me how our hearts were moulded together to work in joint ministry. These were such powerful images at the time, that they stick with me today and I enjoy remembering them.

> # *Activation 10*
> # ***For married couples:***
> *Allow 5-10 minutes for this activation*
>
> - *Find a peaceful place, where you won't be disturbed, and sit comfortably;*
> - *Agree together that you'd like to see The Garden of each other's hearts;*
> - *Have pen and paper/journal to hand;*
> - *Sit together quietly and comfortably;*
> - *Surrender your faith imaginations to the Lord;*
> - *Ask Holy Spirit to show you The Garden of your spouse's heart;*
> - *Be still and receptive;*
> - *Write down any impressions you have;*
> - *Ask questions of the Lord;*
> - *Share your discoveries with each other.*
>
> *Don't be surprised if you find that your spouse's impression of The Garden of your heart is different to your own experience and vice versa. Thank God for these differences and view them as additional dimensions; like double portions.*

If negative aspects crop up during the previous activation, immediately hand them over to the Lord to deal with. Remember that all positives come from God and all negatives come from an accusing enemy. 'We embrace who we face' (Pierce 2014), so face God and ask Him to bring His healing. Wait until it comes. If peace and rest doesn't come by the end of the ten-minute session, it's worth sharing your impressions with your spouse, so that you can prayerfully seek a way forward for you both. Negatives may indicate baggage that hasn't yet been dealt with, e.g. ungodly behaviours, past trauma or spiritual attack; all of which may require deeper ministry (see a list of counselling ministries on page 117)

Chapter 6

The Garden in Times of Trouble

*'He makes me lie down in green pastures, He leads me beside quiet waters,
He refreshes my soul.'*
(Psalm 23:2-3)

I was first struck by the power of Psalm 23 as a child, through watching an old black-and-white film on TV. A frightened nun, in one particular scene, recited aloud the words of this psalm, as if to ward off an approaching enemy. Although I didn't read the Bible as a child, church attendance and church school must have contributed to the familiarity I had with the psalm. But it was more than a passing knowledge of these words of David, that captivated me that day; it was the way the words carried an authority and a truth, that made me feel that I too might find protection, through speaking those words aloud in times of trouble.

Eventually, I did find and learn Psalm 23. I discovered that being able to declare it aloud from memory was definitely a more powerful experience than reading it silently from the page. This isn't very surprising when you consider that when God spoke, in Genesis, the Earth was created; that's because His word is living and active. When we speak God's Word into the atmosphere, something changes in that environment; for when the Word goes out from the mouths of those who love Him, it does not return empty, but will 'achieve the purpose for which [God] sent it' (Isaiah 55:11).

While Psalm 23 can be considered to be a scripture that is particularly apt for those in fear of death, it is a lynchpin scripture for us all as we travel this journey we call life. When you undergo the grief of losing someone close to you, you realise that Psalm 23 is speaking very clearly to those left behind. But it also has a large part to play in helping us find comfort in any difficult situation, whether death is involved or not. Grief comes in many forms and with a variety of causes. The very nature of Psalm 23 provides us with a pastoral backdrop, against which we can find spiritual garden tools to help us in the middle of crises; tools such as God's presence, protection, provision, rest, peace, restoration, direction, righteousness, confidence, comfort, sustenance, anointing, filling, assurance, goodness, love, mercy and hope. What follows is an activation in *lectio divina*, with deep focus from the *inside* of Psalm 23. No matter what you have been through in life so far, there is a place for you in Psalm 23 and the Lord will speak to you clearly as you immerse yourself in its landscape.

Psalm 23:

'The LORD is my shepherd, I lack nothing.
   He makes me lie down in green pastures,
He leads me beside quiet waters, He refreshes my soul.
   He guides me along the right path for His name's sake.
Even though I walk through the darkest valley,
   I will fear no evil,
You are with me; Your rod and your staff,
   they comfort me.
You prepare a table before me
   in the presence of my enemies.
You anoint my head with oil; my cup overflows.
Surely Your goodness and love will follow me
   all the days of my life,
and I will dwell in the house of the LORD forever.'

Activation 11
Experiencing Psalm 23 from the inside
Allow 10 to 20 minutes for this lectio divina activation

Ask Holy Spirit to be with you and lead you in this activation. Then read aloud Psalm 23 on the opposite page and repeat, taking particular note of the landscape of Psalm 23 and what happens in it.

Finally, close your eyes and imagine yourself walking in the landscape of Psalm 23, with Jesus as your shepherd.

- *What strikes you?*
- *Where are you in this landscape?*
- *What are you doing in this landscape?*
- *Where is Jesus in this landscape?*
- *What is Jesus doing in this landscape?*
- *What is Jesus saying in this landscape?*
- *What do you want to say to Jesus in this landscape?*

Either write as you go along or as soon as you finish; otherwise it is easy to forget the finer details.

Re-read your journal notes at a later time. It is likely that there will be elements you will have forgotten, simply because the experience is so deep.

Endeavour to learn this psalm if you don't already know it off by heart.

The rewards of learning Scripture:
When we know God's word by heart, something changes in our spirit. The memorising process helps to etch the Word in our hearts and minds. It is this spiritual engraving that enables deeper personal renewal and a more profound knowledge of God. Learning Scripture from memory may seem daunting, but memorising is like a muscle; it simply has to be used to grow and it gets easier the more you practise. Furthermore, when you start to learn Scripture, you begin to realise that everything in the Bible interrelates; scripture starts to resonate with other scripture and you begin to feel just how alive and active God's Word really is.

The paradox is that, because God has already put His Word in our hearts and minds, as revealed by Jeremiah 31:33, it is as if memorising Scripture activates what God has already planted in us. As a rule, I tend only to learn Scripture according to God's leading. Once, He asked me to learn Isaiah 54. I complained that it was too long and would take a lot of work. "You know it already", came the surprise reply. After thinking about this for a moment, I agreed that I would cover the words on the page with my hand and try to guess what each line of the chapter might say. I shocked myself when I was able to give quite an accurate idea of what each line contained. And so I came to the startling conclusion that God really has written His Word in our hearts and it's all there for us to access. Even so, starting to memorise the scriptures God asks you to learn is a good key to unlocking this great storehouse.

Learning to walk in Scripture as territory:
Learning how to walk in Scripture, just as you have done in previous activations, and owning it as part of your garden in God, feels even more powerful than speaking The Word into the atmosphere. There's nothing quite like actually "being there" to really get to know and understand a locality. While geography can teach us about different physical landscapes and environments, actually going to those places adds depth of understanding that learning on the page doesn't bring. Similarly, while we can read the Bible on the page, it's by actually "going there" and spending time in God's presence, through our faith imagination, that we deepen our understanding of Him and His will for us.

The next activation, across the page, is designed to make Psalm 23 even more your own. As you make yourself at home in this location, and write your own experiences of this Psalm's territory, the power of the space you occupy there will become more a part of you. It will reinforce, intensify and consolidate the Word of God within you.

> ### *Activation 12*
> ### ***Making Psalm 23 personal***
> *Allow 20-30 minutes for this activation*
>
> - *Ask Holy Spirit to be with you and lead you in this activation;*
> - *Rewrite Psalm 23 in your own words;*
> - *Use the notes that you kept from the previous activation on Psalm 23;*
> - *Add your own 'minds-eye' experiences to the mix. This makes Psalm 23 personal to you and helps you to expand this heavenly territory in The Garden of your heart.*

I didn't always believe I had a garden inside me. I suspect that it was William P. Young's (2008) novel, *The Shack*, that triggered such a foundational idea. In the book, Mack's internal struggles are externalised by way of an apparently physical garden, which Holy Spirit tells him is wild, wonderful and perfectly in process; even though it looks messy and lacking order. This garden is a metaphor for Mack's heart; it is his garden of grief for his little murdered daughter.

When my late husband died in 2011, I was already booked to attend a Jesus Ministry conference in London, run by Christ Church Fulham. In my journal at the time, there is a record of a prayer counselling session I received while there, in which I was encouraged to picture myself with Jesus. The scene I imagined was so strong that it has stuck with me to this day and this manual begins with a description of that very picture. Here is what I saw: 'I am in a grassy meadow; there is a red gingham tablecloth on the grass on which is set a wonderful picnic and Jesus is waiting for me; I am neither too late nor too early'. At the time, it felt slightly like *Alice In Wonderland*. Now I can clearly see the Psalm 23 references in it, with its green pasture and lavish feast.

While at the same conference, my assigned counsellor used another strategy with me. It involved me imagining me and God as animals. I remember seeing God as a big, brown, grizzly bear and me as a tiny kitten. Once we had established that the bear would not destroy me, because quite clearly He looked capable of such a thing, I was advised to play as often as I wanted—as a kitten with the bear. And I did, during my quiet times before work, walking over his tummy and tickling Him with my little claws.

Over the next year of grief, whenever I played with the bear, I saw us together in a dark, enclosed wood with seemingly no way out. It felt like a place of seclusion, which mirrored the separateness I felt in early grief; shock and loneliness, in those initial days of mourning, can make one feel alienated from a world that appears to carry on regardless. There were times when I longed to leave this wood, to be free from the dark canopy. Yet, it remained the same for what seemed like quite a long time, until one day, quite unexpectedly, I stepped out of the wood onto a frozen mountain ridge in full sunlight. The next challenge was crossing that ridge, with death-defying drops on either side. As with Song of Songs, explored in chapter 5, every new beginning in God starts with a fresh challenge.

That stage marked the beginning of a very steep learning curve in knowing God, before which I had been relatively incurious about Him and only half committed in my walk with Him. I would honestly, but stubbornly, sing "Here I am, *partially* available for You". I knew I should be wholly available for the Lord, but I just couldn't muster the wherewithal to be so.

One thing I thought worth copying down in my journal, soon after Graham's death, was this: 'Casual prayer gets casual revelation' and 'We need to hunger for God's revelation, not just assume that God knows our address and will send it if He wants. BE CURIOUS!' I had indeed been all too casual in my approach to God. Now I wanted to co-labour with Him, but it was like starting anew. So, armed with the training notes from the Jesus Ministry conference, I undertook serious "stronghold-breaking" activations, exchanging my negative thinking for God's positives, reading all kinds of Christian books and studying the Bible in a new light. Then, *The Garden* began to creep in all by itself.

Three months after Graham died, I wrote this:

> *'Marriage is like a garden. Husband and wife are the gardeners. Both cultivate their own individual plots in the garden around the peripheries and these bloom and grow as the gardeners help each other. But the crowning glory is the central patch that they cultivate together. Any negative aspects go into the compost and the matured compost gets thrown onto the flower beds to make the fertile patches grow even better. So when one gardener dies, the garden still remains. The lost gardener's plot gets chopped down and replanted with small annuals, but the other parts of the garden continue to bloom and grow because of what the lost gardener has contributed for however many years. Those years are not lost.'*

In the centre of this garden, grown by me and Graham, grow two flowers: a large white dahlia, with tightly-packed petals, and a large pink lily, with projecting stamens and anthers. These flowers represent my two grown-up daughters:

The sense of spiritual isolation, in those early weeks of grief, ran in tandem with God's amazing comfort. Initially, my mind's eye often found myself alone in a small tent, with Jesus' nose gently pushed through the entry flaps. That's all that filled the entire entrance of the tent; Jesus' nose! His nose simply touched my nose and we remained that way for some time. I love the image below, because it speaks of the tenderness, proximity and depth of God's comfort at a time of deep sorrow. I told my church curate of this experience and she replied "Jesus must have a really big nose!" And, apparently, He does!

The wonder of God's vengeance in Isaiah 61:2 is that it does not bring the kind of destruction the word earthly 'vengeance' seems to indicate. Rather, God's vengeance is to destroy the work of the enemy, by comforting all who mourn and providing for those who grieve. In Isaiah 61:3, He does the divine exchange in grief: the crown of beauty instead of ashes, the oil of joy instead of mourning and a garment of praise instead of despair. Then, in the same verse, those who mourn become oaks of righteousness; a great planting for the display of God's splendour. Thus, in Isaiah 61:4, when God's comfort is added to grief, the result is strong and mighty trees which not only bring glory to God, but go on to rebuild, restore and renew all that has previously been devastated. What a healing paradox! What a mighty garden is the heart that walks through grief and out the other side!

My artistic impression of Jesus' comforting nose

Interestingly, during the months after Graham's death, a number of people came to tell me of dreams and visions they'd had of Graham. A recurring theme was a picture of Graham sat in wonder in the middle of a flower meadow, which resonates with Heaven as a garden. Rather mysteriously, all these people were called either Graham or Ruth, which indicates a very deliberate intentionality in the way God chose to communicate with me at that time.

I have never been more aware that I am made of three parts than in those early months of grief. It felt like a great explosion had taken place, with the pieces of my life seemingly spinning around me; like smouldering shrapnel, eventually coming to rest on the ground around my feet. As far as my body was concerned, it went on strike and I was unable to eat. Meanwhile my mind was constantly racing, maelstrom like, as I tried to deal with all that had to be done with the vast changes that ensued. But my spirit was somewhere else. My spirit was soaring, unencumbered by my fractured body and mind. My spirit broke free into a level of communion with God I'd never experienced before. Below is my artistic impression of what it felt like:

My artistic impression of the explosion of grief

Two years after Graham died, I went to see his tombstone; finally in situ at the cemetery. I was alone and wept down the phone to Ray, whom I'd been dating for six months. A strange thing happened, as we prayed on the phone; in my mind's eye, I saw Graham standing in green pastures by still waters, as if in Psalm 23. He was dressed in a smart dark suit and he looked over the water, with his back towards me. "What shall I do?" I enquired of the Lord. "Take his hand." So I quietly approached the silent figure and held his left hand in my right. Neither of us spoke. Jesus had already made it privately clear to me five months earlier that Ray was to be my next husband and, in my mind's eye, I turned to hold Ray's hand as well. But, you can't have two husbands. In order to become Ray's wife, I needed to take him with both hands and this meant letting go Graham.

Only later did I learn about spiritual soul ties between people (for more on this, see pages 105-108); these are generally good when it comes to active and healthy family relationships, but need breaking when a relationship ends through death or divorce. Then a person is much more able to enter into the next chapter of their lives, without being encumbered by previously shared spiritual "substance". The Lord helped me to navigate this task with enormous gentleness, using the still waters of Psalm 23 as that touching place where the heavenly meets the earthly. And, as if sensing my new spiritual freedom, Ray declared his love for me three days later.

I still return to Psalm 23 on a regular basis. It offers so much for all kinds of scenarios in life. The pasture can be a place of rest and restoration, but also a place to simply pass time with the Lord. The straight and right path is always about aligning oneself to God's thinking, capturing every thought and enquiring of next steps. The valley can represent our whole life journey, as well as specific times of difficulty. When it feels dark, Jesus leads us through, always tapping His rod against the rock to reassure us of His presence with us.

Always, there is the picnic with the red gingham cloth laid out and Jesus sitting there laughing and relaxed, giving no mind to the enraged enemy melting into the background. Here, Jesus repeatedly anoints my head with oil. My glass of heavenly wine is always full and over flowing, because it represents the power of His life-giving blood; shed on the cross in order to give us life in all its fullness. Because He works good in all things for those that love Him, no matter what is thrown my way I know that His goodness and mercy will never leave me. Knowing these things centres me and helps me not only to remain standing upright on life's tightrope, but to walk at higher levels and advance forward without fear of falling. There is always more with God.

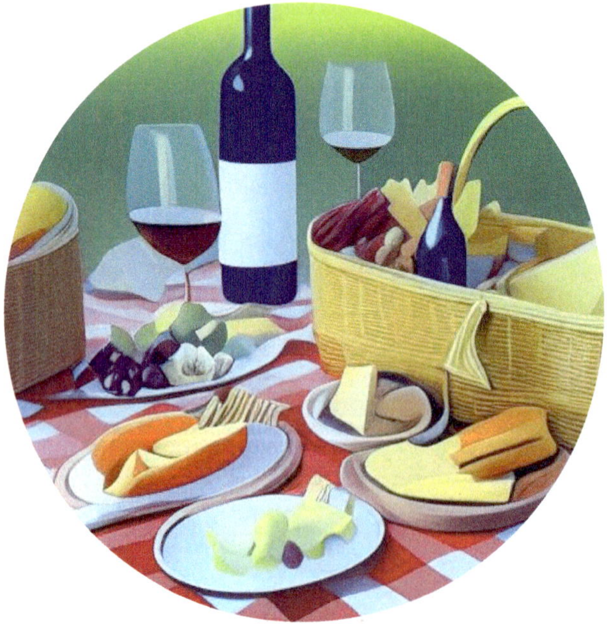

Chapter 7

The Ever Expanding Garden

'The kingdom is not discovered in one place or another, for God's kingdom realm is already expanding within some of you.'
(Luke 17:21, The Passion Translation, 2020)

Enlarge the place of your tent:
God always sees the bigger picture so when He asks us to enlarge the place of our tent, in Isaiah 54:2, He's making it clear that we are always in need of more expansion into His territory. In the book of Isaiah, God is calling His nation back to Him, as a husband calls back a deserted and distressed wife. However, Isaiah doesn't just speak to the Jews of his day, but to future generations of all people in the world, who are willing to respond to the loving call of their Maker (see Isaiah 2:2-5, 56:3-8 and 60:3-5). In the Old Covenant, tents portray the dwelling places of God's people and tent enlargement the taking back of earthly territory with spiritual benefits. At that time, domestic tents were considered quite distinct from the sanctified tent or tabernacle, which was the forerunner of the temple in Jerusalem; the place in which the Lord's presence rested amongst His people. Furthermore, the temple was a representation of the Garden of Eden before The Fall (Sobel, 2022). It was Pentecost which brought the prophecy of Ezekiel 37:26-28 into being and, through the cross and resurrection, God has put His sanctuary and His garden among us forever; by putting them *in* us.

This necessitates seeing tent expansion with new eyes. 2 Corinthians 5:1-4 and 1 Corinthians 6:19-20 describe our physical bodies as tents. They are not just temporary dwelling places, but temples of the Holy Spirit. So, while humankind began as chosen and created, born into God's Kingdom, now God's Kingdom has been born into His chosen ones, making them new creations. This demonstrates the means by which God will fulfil the prophecy of Joel 2:28, when He will finally 'pour out [His] Spirit on all flesh'. But because there is always "the more" of God, expansion of God's Kingdom will not just be through increased numbers of Spirit-filled people but through Kingdom expansion within us.

With the Kingdom expanding within us, it is obviously not our physical bodies we want to enlarge in order to increase our capacity for God. The tent the Father is referring to is the tabernacle kind; the one in our heart/spirit. Such spiritual growth resonates with Job 36:16, which speaks of God wooing us 'to a spacious place, free from restriction'. With Holy Spirit within us, *The Garden* helps us to see that we are bigger on the inside than on the outside and have permission to grow into all that Heaven has for us, right here and right now. Because that's a lot to take in, God gives us the ability to take possession of this amazing inheritance a bit at a time and *The Garden* of our heart is a tool that helps us to become proactive in this venture.

Expansion through coming alive to God:
The combination of practising being in the Lord's presence and capturing every thought to the obedience of God is often known as "dying to self". But this process runs in tandem with "coming alive to God" or "waking up to God", like the Bride of Song of Songs. The wonder of dying to our old self, is that our true self blossoms in the presence of the Lord. The light of our God-given identity blots out the shadows of our old character, which has been disconnected from our Maker and is therefore dead. And it is our true "original design" which truly glorifies the Lord, because that is the image of Himself that He has planted within us. As we grow, we resonate more with God and consequently have more to reflect back to Him. Therefore, it's not so much a matter of "more of God and less of me," but a case of "more of God and more of the true me in God".

Opposite is an optical analogy to demonstrate this truth. Imagine the true self as being the interior of an eye ball. The pupil represents the old, false self. Looking from the outside, the black pupil appears to almost eclipse the heavenly treasure that God has planted within. While bright natural light enters a biological eye from the outside, causing the earthly pupil to contract to pin-point size, the heavenly flips that around and works from the inside out. As new creations, we have the light of God's glory within us, by way of Holy Spirit. As we tune in more and more to Holy Spirit living within us, we respond less and less to natural stimuli. In the presence of God's light within, it is as if the dark pupil of the old self must surrender its natural instinct to constrict and, instead, dilate wider and wider until it is finally invisible. While the true self appears to grow bigger and the old self smaller, actually the dying, soulish self just uncovers what was already there, making it more evident as we grow into God's spaciousness. To all appearances, it does look like the Kingdom of God enlarging within us.

As we grow into God's spaciousness, the old, false self gradually disappears

Such growth necessitates seeing ourselves as God sees us and aligning our thoughts with His. The expansion process grinds to a halt when we focus mainly on our sin or worthlessness and see ourselves as unlovable, dirty rags rather than the Bride of Christ, who is actually adorned beautifully in robes of Christ's righteousness. As a friend so aptly said to me recently, Jesus' robes of righteousness dress us on the inside as well as on the outside, so that we have no need to feel we are hiding dirty secrets beneath the folds. Graham Cooke (2023) repeatedly reminds us that "Grace is the empowering presence of God, that enables you to become the person that He sees when He looks at you, in Jesus." We all trip up, but like a toddler who falls and hurts themself, we get back up again. Just like the Bride of Song of Songs, we develop Godly strategies and resilience for getting through the difficulties, because we're not doing it alone. When we accept that there is no condemnation in Christ, that's when we can get big with God. Our faith imagination is a tool for creating the space for these processes to unfold.

There is always more with God. When in *The Garden* I once asked Jesus how many dimensions there are and He replied, "Well, there's the first and the second and the third and the fourth and the fifth and the sixth and the seventh..."; I got the idea that eternity's dimensions are never ending. There is so much more to come.

Ever-increasing circles:
Development in God takes place in a kind of spiral curriculum, in which we enlarge in ever-increasing circles; simultaneously living our lives and expanding into God. Through journaling and repeated visits to *The Garden*, I have learnt to appreciate God's love of circles and cycles. Life on Earth has numerous cycles built into it, but so does Life in the Spirit. This kind of progression may involve repeated visitations to similar situations; not because we are pointlessly going round and round in circles, but because

it's a demonstration of how we have expanded in faith and belief to become bigger than the circumstances. So while Earth remains the same size, despite the ebb and flow of her tides and change of seasons, in the Spirit we are meant to grow exponentially. In the last book of the Narnia Series (Lewis, 2009), the writer describes going deeper into Heavenly territory as going 'further up and further in'; higher and deeper. This is certainly what *The Garden* encourages.

I find chapters one and ten in Ezekiel helpful when imagining how we grow in God. While this scripture is more about a mobile Heaven than a garden, using one's faith imagination to take possession of this particular vision can have remarkable results. So a *lectio divina* exercise with these two chapters comes highly recommended. Why not take a look at Ezekiel chapters one and ten for yourself, before reading on?

When I read Ezekiel 1 and 10, I see myself standing in the middle of the burning coals, given access by what Jesus has done on the cross; I feel strongly that Jesus is represented by the man, of Ezekiel 10:2-7, dressed in linen. The fire represents Holy Spirit, as well as God's ability to continually purify me. I am surrounded by the four cherubim and see all their four faces as being different representations of Jesus: the man, the ox of sacrifice, the Lion of Judah and the eagle of prophecy; prophecy being the testimony of Jesus (Revelation 19:10). I imagine Jesus in front of me, the ox to my right, the lion to my left and the eagle behind me. The cherubim are very large and their all-seeing wings touch to form a vast tent around me. The all-seeing gyroscopic wheels of chrysolite move with the cherubim. Above me is the sea of glass, like a ceiling.

In my heavenly imagination, I grow and grow and, as I do so, the cherubim grow with me to what seems like 200 foot. As a result, the tent of their wings around me also enlarges, to accommodate my growth. It's as if the fire below inflates me, as heat expands air, and I'm aware of growing outwards as well as upwards. Finally, I break through the surface of the sea of glass to see The Almighty on His sapphire/lapis lazuli throne, surrounded by the emerald rainbow. As I come up through the waters, I see that many others are also surfacing. It is as if the sea dresses us in one unifying, watery and heavenly robe. Spiritual growth helps us break through and brings us closer not only to God's throne but to one another. As I work with this visualisation, it is as if the elements in this scripture form mighty spiritual armour. It surrounds me on all sides, as well as below and above; growing with me as I develop.

My "spiral-curriculum" development regarding the armour of God began as a very young Christian. Then the name of Jesus protected me, but I had no awareness of Ephesians 6:10-18 (see page 113). A few years later, this spiritual armour was brought to my attention and I was advised to put it on daily. Later, I realised that when I allowed Jesus to dress me in my armour, it doesn't fall off (see page 44). For years I've lived in the armour of the mobile throne-room, as witnessed by Ezekiel, which expands as I grow. At the moment, I am growing into sapphire pavement territory.

The spirit-to-soul feedback loop:
As already explained on page 29, the brain has neuroplastic abilities, in which visualisation can help to create new nerve pathways and new thoughts over time (Zoe, 2023). In Jeremiah 31:33, when the Lord pledges to put His law in His people's minds and hearts, God reveals His heavenly enlargement plans not only for the mind but for the heart as well; something which Joel 2:28 confirms is for all people. In Matthew 22:37-40, Jesus makes it clear that the two greatest commandments in the law of Moses are to love God and to love others. All this is possible because God 'first loved us' (1 John 4:19). One depends upon the other and requires continual flow from our Creator. Spiritual enlargement can only come by staying connected to God's perfect love, no matter what has happened in our lives.

Consequently, when we surrender our brains to God's plans and love for us, and proactively co-labour with Him, a heavenly feedback loop is created between spirit and soul. The presence of God in our hearts sends spiritual stimuli to refresh the hardware of our brain, which in turn sends renewed stimuli to all the parts of our soul: mind, emotions and will. This feedback loop is all part and parcel of the heavenly spiral curriculum of learning. *The Garden* is a tool which can help build such heavenly highways and spiritual muscle. It may be a leisurely, drip-by-drip approach to healing, but it is gentle, relatively pain free and has the advantage of offering total confidentiality between us and God.

Recognising vicious circles:
When life does not follow a path of increasing spiritual expansion, elements of failure and unhappiness often mirror internal roadblocks to development. A life that's got stuck like this is a red flag for some kind of inner misalignment and a symptom that cries out to be resolved. Even with Christians, unsettled hurts—as awful as child abuse or as normal as sibling rivalry in childhood—can be a spanner in a person's soul. Such pain can jangle noisily in thoughts and feelings, which seem to continuously distract a person away from Holy Spirit's voice and direction. Christine Wren James' (2014) book, *Naked I Stand*, tells her own story of being abused and helps the reader to recognise and deal with past pain, in order to move forward into all that God has planned for them.

I used to pray regularly with a friend I'll call Andrea. When we looked over everything that had happened to her in her recent life, I could see that she was repeatedly returning to square one without much obvious growth; it was as if she kept hitting the same buffers. Everywhere she went, she felt victimised. I drew her a picture of many hurdles in a line and asked her if she felt she was forever having to jump exactly the same hurdle. She readily agreed. Instead of ever increasing circles of growth, she was experiencing a vicious cycle. I suggested inner healing, but at that time, she was unwilling to pray through the strongholds on her life and has now left the area. My prayer is that one day she will find the healing, peace and acceptance that has always been hers to claim.

It's hard when hurts create unhelpful, self-protective responses, which dig ruts of self-defeating thought processes. This takes us back to Paul's directive to 'take every thought captive', in 2 Corinthians 10:5. If we include emotions with thoughts, it is possible for us to arrest negative, painful thoughts and emotions that, by their nature, set themselves up against God's Word and will for our lives. Once captured, the root cause can be dealt with in the moment and surrendered to God. The new pathway is revealed by way of the divine exchange, in which we replace the hurt with God's promises of healing, protection and love (see page 139 for fifteen promises of God). Most negative thoughts need dealing with repeatedly until they finally dissipate, in exchange for the re-laid, heavenly path.

Chapter 8

Others' Experiences of *The Garden*

*'You who dwell in the gardens with friends in attendance,
let me hear your voice!'
(Songs of Songs 8:13)*

Over the years, I've shared my experiences of *The Garden* with those close to me, as well as leading others into *The Gardens* of their own hearts through dedicated sessions at Norfolk Healing Rooms and Norfolk School of Prophets. Feedback from group work exploring *The Garden* tends to be full of excitement at the immediacy of such encounters with Jesus, so readily and beautifully connecting people's hearts to God. The resulting revelations stir the spirit and spark new beginnings in us. The following are personal accounts from people who have given permission for me to share their encounters in *The Garden*.

Feedback from a small-group session in *The Garden*:

The following four write ups came about from a small-group, "garden" session at Norfolk School of Prophets (NSOP), by way of Zoom.

Michael's experience of *The Garden*:
"In this Zoom session, Ruth invited us to experience a prophetic activation, in which we were all encouraged to visit *The Garden* of our hearts. I had never done this before and I write the following from notes I made as I walked through this encounter.

I looked at a picture on screen of a beautiful gate, which was fully open, and gave me a glimpse into the entrance of an English, red-bricked, walled garden. I was encouraged to ask Jesus a question, so I said "What would You like to do, Jesus?" I sensed Him answer with a question, as He asked me "Can I come into your garden?" and I replied "Yes" ('I have come into my garden, my sister, my bride,' Song of Songs 5:1). I held His hand, imagining Him on my right side, and we walked in together.

It was a bright day and we were greeted by a beautiful, perfectly square, red-brick, walled garden. In the middle, it had a group of trees of medium width, but tall and planted close and perfectly apart. This tree formation reminded me of a small wooded area next to Willen Lake, in Milton Keynes; I always admired it, when I drove past. In my garden, there was a path bordering the wooded area and a row of flowers, with roses between the path and the wall. They were all in groups of different colours and equal in height. Everything was neat and tidy, reflecting elements of my character; with the need for order and control.

Then I sensed and heard a voice say "Peek a boo!" and I could see someone hiding behind a tree. "Come play with Me! Hide and seek." And I sensed Jesus say, "You're seeing your heart as too small". Suddenly the borders of the walls expanded and the small wooded area became a vast forest, as in Isaiah 54:2-3; 'Enlarge the place of your tent, stretch your tent curtains wide, do not hold back, lengthen your cords, strengthen your stakes.' I now could see a garden of unlimited size. "Come and get lost in My shadow of love," came to mind, as well as, "Rest in My love and relax in My care".

I then heard Ruth talking about our hearts being a healing garden. I started to feel the tangible presence of God and could see *The Garden* fill with cloud. There were different colours flashing within the cloud and I thought of the glory of God.

Ruth also mentioned that we could pose as many questions to Jesus as we liked. I began to think about the challenges of becoming a Funeral Celebrant. Although I didn't speak a word, my thoughts seemed to affect *The Garden* and dark clouds began forming in the sky above us. But I sensed that God dismissed the clouds out of sight, not wanting me to dwell on this or worry about it at all.

I was invited into the forest and I walked in. As I walked further and further in, water began to rise around my body right up to my neck. Everything I could see suddenly turned completely upside down and, as I tried to reason this in my thoughts, I remembered reading in the past that things in the Kingdom of God are upside down in comparison to our way of doing things. I walked forward, out of this place and sensed the Holy Spirit say, "Come out of the darkness, into the light". I could now see a very bright sun in the far distance, with light shining everywhere. I walked into the light and that was the end.

At the close of the Zoom session, my children left the house to drive to a water park activity with the church and I chose to stay behind. I sensed The Holy Spirit beckoning me to spend time with Him. Once alone, I sensed His tangible presence and His desire to dance with me. So we danced to Nat King Cole and again I was reminded of His invitation to come and get lost in His shadow; the shadow of love."

Sandra's experience of *The Garden*:
"I've just listened to the NSOP recording and followed through with going into *The Garden* of my heart with Jesus. In *The Garden* I was sitting by a fountain with Jesus. It was peaceful and refreshing. I was asking Him about the purpose and direction of my life. I was surprised to see there was a windsock in *The Garden*. He showed me that just as a pilot uses a windsock to see speed and direction of the wind, I would be able to see the direction of the wind of Holy Spirit. That would be my guide, so that I would take off to go where He wanted and to land where He wanted. As in Isaiah 30:21 'Whether you turn to the right or to the left, your ears will hear a voice behind you, saying, *This is the way; walk in it.*'"

Jill's experiences of *The Garden*:
"I stood outside the door to *The Garden* and Jesus came and held my hand. This was a very special moment. However, I still hesitated, as I didn't feel that I could go into *The Garden* at all, as I felt I was not worthy. Then God said "Do you love me, Jill? Will you come with me, for I want you to?" He insisted, so I was brave and went inside *The Garden*, because I could feel this love and warmth coming out from there. This impression made me feel that it was a safe thing to do, but still it took quite a lot of courage.

The Garden was a place of encouragement and love and not one of condemnation. My feet took me deeper into *The Garden*. I noticed the wonderful fragrance and the warmth of the sunshine on my skin. I could see masses of blue forget-me-nots growing in rich brown soil. I felt God saying the flowers were small, but not insignificant and should not be overlooked. As He said this, He looked at me meaningfully. Yes I am small, but not insignificant and definitely not overlooked by Him.

As I walked on, I could see lovely, fluffy sheep which made me think of cotton-wool sheep. I came to a forked stick standing in the ground and it seemed to indicate that there were choices of path to take: either the fast-paced, more strenuous route or the slow-paced, steady route. Apparently, I could take either, as they would get me to the same destination. I chose the slow, steady route.

God encouraged me to "Wait and listen." I was surrounded by wonderful sounds of creation: birds, insects, the wind playing with the leaves. I walked on and was again encouraged to "Wait and wonder".

God led me to a sundial. I had a sense that He was saying it was time; time to move into a new phase of my life. It felt awesome!

I returned to *The Garden* at a later date and followed the same path as before. As I was led back to the sundial, I passed a water clock on the way. It was filling and emptying regularly, producing a glorious melody. This time, at the sundial, God said it was time to receive healing from false memories. He reminded me of events, through which He revealed His truth in those situations. He encouraged me to bring my hurts and problems to Him and to wait for Him to reveal His light and truth. And He said this He will do, because He loves me."

Jim's experience of *The Garden*:
"The first time I went into *The Garden*, having never really looked into my heart before, I saw fruit trees. At first glance they appeared empty, but on closer inspection I saw there were lots of low-hanging fruit on them. However, this wasn't what I was being led to, but to a couple of raised beds. They looked like they were being prepared for planting. Jesus took me to one of these prepared beds. For all intents and purposes it looked bare, but He was pointing out one or two green shoots. What Jesus transmitted was excitement for these green sproutings. I began to sense He wanted me to be excited too. Now, the question for me to explore with Him is what these one or two seedlings are about.

The second time I went into *The Garden* of my heart I didn't refer to the first experience as my starting point, and had such a different encounter. As I took Jesus' hand and walked into *The Garden*, through the archway, all went black. I couldn't see a thing. Jesus was still holding my hand, but I couldn't see anything; not even Him. The walk was without fear or anxiety. Despite seeing and hearing nothing, I was at peace.

I asked Jesus, 'If you are the light of the world, the light that shines in the darkness, why can't I see you?' There was no answer. We continued to move forward in silence. There was no sound, not even our footsteps, and yet I still felt peaceful.

Then I was reminded that in Genesis 1, when all the world was dark and formless, Jesus was there. I asked Jesus why He desired to show me this. Jesus answered, 'I was there before all time, but I knew already what it would become; beautiful. Similarly with you, I already knew how beautiful you would become. Do you not perceive it?'

The third time I visited *The Garden* of my heart, it was reminiscent of my first experience. So, as we walked through the archway into *The Garden*, I saw the fruit trees. I asked Jesus if we could go to the prepared bed. When we got there this time, much had changed and the patch was now covered with what appeared to be small, cotton-ball-shaped plants. As I pondered this, Jesus led me to quite a large airy building, built against the wall of *The Garden*. Here, in this warm, bright space, Jesus picked up a flourishing seed tray and showed it to me. He then returned it to its place and led me to another room, where I now saw a bucket being filled with cut flowers that looked like tulips.

I was left with a sense of "Wow! There's a lot going on here!" But I also had questions, as I wondered how much I really see of what's actually going on and how much time I should spend thinking about, reflecting upon and enjoying the processes and stages taking place in *The Garden* of my heart."

More experiences of *The Garden*

My journey through *The Garden* by Glyn:

> 'You are a garden locked up, my sister, my bride;
> you are a spring enclosed, a sealed fountain.'
> *(Song of Songs 4:12)*

"For quite some time, when praying and reading the Bible alone in my flat, I had often visited a peaceful, private garden in my heart to be alone with Jesus. Then one day Ruth and I were talking and Ruth too had been in her own "garden" with Jesus. That discussion made me feel even safer and willing to go deeper into *The Garden*. I became confident that God was indeed the designer and it was not just my own imagination.

To enter *The Garden*, I had walked through a wooden gate and into a bright, open, green field. In the far distance, I could see hills and mountains on my left, a huge, silent waterfall to my right and beautiful trees lined a wide, flowing river.

Always there, in sight, was a very relaxed figure of a man. He would sometimes be sitting on the bank of the river with bare feet, one foot dangling in the water, looking down or crossed legged, looking across the river at the trees. Oftentimes, He was just standing upright. But always looking and waiting; waiting for me!

The very first time, in my heart, I knew who the figure of the man was, but in my head I said "It can't be! And even if it is, I can't go anywhere near Him!"

Sharing with Ruth about our "gardens" gave me enough courage to finally walk towards Him and surrender to His gentle, all encompassing, forgiving love. Initially, I would start to walk slowly towards Him and be held quietly in His arms. We would sit side-by-side together, next to the river, and talk and talk. Other times I would be washed in the river by His angels.

Gradually I began to run, to be caught up laughing in His arms and twirled around like a child. Then maybe walking, held or flying, He would take me towards the waterfall, which roared and foamed as we drew near, soaking us even before we fully reached it.

Behind the waterfall lay a world, which sadly I have neither the words nor talent to describe. In it were no earthly rules and He would soar me heavenwards to view the cities of the world, then later upwards into space to see our beautiful world below and further still out into His incredible endless universe, full of colour and wonder.

My journey into *The Garden* is still evolving, details too deep, intimate and far too long to describe. Our God is an awesome, unfathomable God who is so willing to reach down and take us gently into unexplored lands, if we are open and willing to walk with Him."

Enlarge your heart by Ray:

"Many years ago, I came to realise that my heart was like a garden and I liked the idea that my creative instincts and previous training could be harnessed by that too. At the time, I wondered if I would also need to develop a wild imagination and decided to wait and see. Whatever was to happen, the Holy Spirit would lead; so no striving! *The Garden* is not something that the imagination alone can prise open; it requires the inspiration of the Holy Spirit from the heart.

As I continued to pray for folk, more and more opportunity arose for the Holy Spirit to drop into my mind the prayer with which He wanted to enlarge their hearts and how that could happen. Revelation of God comes in different ways and I found that the more I prayed garden-enlarging prayers into others, the more I began to see different parts of *The Garden* of my own heart. I began to feel more and more comfortable with the prayers and the landscapes they took me into and I could tell this was not mysticism or drug-induced (not that I've ever indulged).

My imaginations take me into large landscapes with fields, seascapes, trees and vast views, which last seconds. It is like the Garden of Eden. It never seems to rain, snow or be windy but is mostly calm and brings solid comfort, healing and certainly peace that passes all understanding. It never gives me the cringe factor. I just believe God is showing me more of His truths and that Heaven is coming down to Earth.

We all need to see spiritually what is legal for us to see, but learned narrowings have held us back. Just because we don't understand, doesn't mean to say it's not God and not true. It has been said that there is a writing, in the Jewish Talmud, which states that we will have to give an account to God of all the permissible pleasures we failed to enjoy on Earth. It's a reminder and a caution against keeping God in a box. As Solomon writes in Proverbs 25:2, 'It is the glory of God to conceal a matter; to search out a matter is the glory of kings'."

Michelle's encounter in *The Garden*:
"I went to the love seat inside my heart where Jesus and I regularly sit. Jesus took me to a dining table for two, in a beautiful forest area. The chairs were ornate and high backed. He pulled out the chair for me to sit on and pushed it to the table. He sat opposite me. As we sat with the food before us, Jesus produced a treasure box which contained all the love letters I've ever written to Him (I have written lots in my journal over the years). He took some out and read them back to me. Tears of joy flowed down my cheeks, as I realised how precious these are to Him.

Next He showed me His treasure box for me. As I peered in, it looked empty! BUT, as I put my hand in, it was full of life. He said "What would you like to put in it? You can choose." I could see the life and energy within the box, it contained miraculous life-giving energy; limitless and indescribable. As I put my hand in, I could go in—fully. Somehow it expanded to fit me in. It unveiled me, enfolded in His glory and life; covered, filled, energised and free. Full of life I can go anywhere, fulfil His perfect will for me and in His authority. Wow!"

Chapter 9

The Garden as a Ministry Tool for Facilitators and Ministers

"You will be like a well-watered garden."
(Isaiah 58:11)

The Garden and the imagination can be good tools for ministering healing to those who seek restoration or simply "the more" of God. *The Garden* works best in small groups, with couples or on a one-to-one basis. When led by Holy Spirit, I frequently use *The Garden* to help people to find rest, healing or answers and it is particularly helpful for finding relief and direction in the middle of deep strife. Not only is it beautifully evocative, but it encourages encounter with the living God, which is always healing. Furthermore, because the person seeking healing is the explorer in this heavenly territory, they have a great deal of agency at a time when they may well feel trapped by their circumstances. So it's good, as a healing minister, to see oneself simply as a facilitator; deferring to Holy Spirit at all times, in a process that allows the explorer to be led and taught by the Lord.

A person in need of ministry calls for a confident, knowledgeable prayer minister. It might be obvious to say that, to use *The Garden* as a ministry tool, a facilitator needs to be very familiar not only with the gardens of Eden, Psalm 23 and Song of Songs but also of their own heart; not to mention a good working knowledge of the Bible. The biggest challenge for a facilitator is coming up against an explorer's resistance to entering *The Garden*; through fear, grief, low self esteem, feeling overwhelmed by their situation or other causes. This is when experience of *The Garden*, scriptural knowledge and spiritual maturity all help a prayer minister find inspired ways of encouraging breakthrough.

Ideally, a "garden" session with a facilitator will stimulate the explorer to start utilising *The Garden* as a regular, daily, brief intervention for themselves, as part of their regular quiet time. Learning requires repetition and perseverance. One visit to *The Garden* may be a lovely experience, but many visits increase the chances of healing and spiritual growth. However, a counsellor said some very helpful words to me at the end of my session with her: "Play there as often as you want to." This emphasises the joyful and voluntary elements of going to *The Garden*. It shouldn't feel like hard work that's being imposed; that's no fun at all. And it's the fun that helps with the learning.

Psalm 23 as an activation in a small group:
Practising *lectio divina* with Psalm 23, when led by Holy Spirit, is the most straightforward garden to use in ministry. There is an activation for a personal trip through Psalm 23 on page 63 and the approach is similar for a group. Even if people have only a sketchy knowledge of the Bible, most are familiar with the kind of concepts that abound in Psalm 23: bodies of water, green fields, paths, valleys, food and drink.

When leading a group of people, the facilitator will first establish the importance of confidentiality, in order to create a safe space. Then they will invite Holy Spirit to go before them. If the session is on Zoom, they might want to share a picture that brings Psalm 23 to mind. The next step is for the folk to read Psalm 23 before closing their eyes and imagining

themselves, as David did, walking through the Psalm's terrain. It's key to allow sufficient time for this to happen. Twenty minutes is usually enough for most people, but it's good to be prepared to give extra time to those who haven't quite finished at the same juncture as everyone else.

When completed, the group is encouraged to write down elements that struck them most as they journeyed through the Psalm. If individuals are willing, these exploits can be shared with the group. No doubt people will have similar confirmatory experiences, as well as very different encounters. This highlights that while we do have shared spiritual awareness, we are also very diverse and at different points on our journeys in life and with the Lord.

What excites most people is that they have an actual encounter with the living God in this activation, with true revelation of how He sees them and how He is working in their lives. The sharing of these discoveries highlights God's ability to meet each person exactly where they are, even in such a group of assorted personalities. As a facilitator, it's good to rejoice with those who share their discoveries. Small breakthroughs can lead to huge spiritual advances.

Psalm 23 as an activation with an individual or couple:
There's a different approach when dealing with one person or a married couple, when it is much more like a counselling session. The facilitator will be listening for spiritual direction even before meeting the individual(s), taking notes for use in the session.

After that, the first requirement is a private and comfortable place to sit, with a couple of hours available. With the person/couple put at ease, they are given space to vocalise their reason for attending. The facilitator is in proactive listening mode and may take occasional contemporaneous written notes, with the permission of the guest(s). Proactive listening not only involves taking notice of what is being said, but also pays attention to what Holy Spirit is revealing. The Lord will make it clear, before or during the session, that Psalm 23 is indicated and He will bring to the fore anything that particularly strikes a chord from what is said by the guest(s).

Once the person/couple has finished telling their story, the facilitator explains to them that they are going to explore psalm 23. Holy Spirit is invited to lead all explorations through the Psalm. You can use a picture to help them visualise. There is no one way of approach, because Holy Spirit tailors *The Garden* for each individual, so it's good to be sensitive to the Spirit's leading. I tend to ask the explorer(s) to close their eyes while I read Psalm 23 aloud, adjusted so that I make it specific to them, i.e. "The Lord is *your* shepherd". Essentially, it is like a soaking session, in which they relax and immerse themselves in the Word. Then I invite them to take their time in wandering around the terrain of Psalm 23, in their mind's eye, identifying the Lord in that landscape and looking for extras—anything in their imagination that is not specifically mentioned in the Psalm.

Silence is something facilitators can find difficult, but waiting in silence is what allows space and time for something to happen in the explorer's spirit. Patience is a heavenly fruit, especially when exercised in these circumstances. It's prudent to remember that this is the explorer's journey and not that of the facilitator, even though the prayer minister may be quietly walking alongside the guest in their own mind's eye.

Furthermore, in this silence, there are clues that can indicate to the facilitator that something is taking place. So, it's the facilitator's job to proactively watch out for subtle changes in the explorer's facial expressions: flickering eyelashes, smiles, tears, sighs etc. Most healing ministries teach their prayer counsellors to keep their eyes open, so as not to miss anything.

Then it is the facilitator's job to discern exactly when to step in and find out what's actually happening, in order to assess progress. The whole session may involve a series of repeated silences, each followed by a few questions; silence allowing the explorer to travel and the facilitator's questions creating stepping stones to help consolidate each experience before moving on.

Open questions are vital here. Questions that require "Yes/No" replies can limit the explorer's freedom to explain, describe and expand. So, at what is perceived to be the right time, the facilitator may simply ask "What's happening?" If Jesus is identified as being visible in the imagined terrain, the explorer may be asked to approach Him. After a pause, the explorer may be invited to explain if anything else is taking place, what they and Jesus are doing, if anything is being said and how they are feeling.

Allowing the explorer to journey unimpeded is an approach very much to be fostered. Being too directive or prescriptive can very quickly close down a session in *The Garden*, by wresting control from the Spirit and giving the explorer a sense of being manipulated. I try not to suggest what an explorer should do, even if I have a clear picture in my own mind's eye of what the explorer is doing or saying in *The Garden*. After all, if appropriate, this can be shared afterwards. However, if the explorer has got stuck and can't seem to proceed, I may then make a suggestion as a gentle nudge to help them progress.

I had one lady, whom I'll call Faith, who was grieving. She was keen for a "garden" session and together we agreed that we would focus on Psalm 23. Faith had no problem at all imagining herself sitting against a tree with Jesus, on a high ridge above an area reminiscent of the Lake District. It was beautiful, peaceful, safe and restful. She was reclining in the green pastures of Psalm 23 and it was where she needed to be.

Afterwards, I expressed to Faith my surprise at her being able to be in such a high place at such a difficult time, especially as we were focussing on Psalm 23 with its dark valley. I made the observation that the still waters of Psalm 23, so needed in grief, were down in the valley far away from her. Still water is God's way of breaking down the great ocean of grief into manageable portions. Faith paused and then explained that she had heard a podcast about people who get stuck in the valley of grief, so she was determined that she wasn't going to do that.

Now, I don't want anyone to be unhappy, but grief is like a territory of sadness that simply has to be walked '*through*' (Psalm 23:4), in order to get to the other side; it is a realm that has to be conquered before a person can move on to the next area of life, which God has prepared for them. A mourner can choose to block out grief; thereby skirting around the territory which has been assigned to them to take and liberate. Nevertheless, it will remain unconquered land, which will be a bane for as long as it remains enemy-occupied.

Because God's great vengeance against the enemy is to bring comfort to those who mourn (Isaiah 61:2 and Matthew 5:4), it could be said that the enemy in the valley of Psalm 23 is grief itself. When a mourner co-labours with the Lord, they receive all God's good travelling gifts for the journey of sorrow, as described in Psalm 23. With God they can get through to the other side and experience a complete reversal of grief's hardships, through the divine exchange, referred to in Isaiah 61:3. Then not only do they conquer grief, but they become rebuilders of hope, dressed in royal robes of beauty, joy and praise. The result sees them so rooted in and made right by the Lord, that they are like resilient, fruitful and Spirit-filled oaks.

The penny dropped for Faith. She made the connection with the still waters of Psalm 23 and realised how far away they were in her current situation in *The Garden*. However, God meets us exactly where we are and we agreed that Faith needed to be just where she was on the high ridge top, for the moment; because that was where Jesus had made her lie down. However, she began to see that she should not need to be afraid of the time to come when Jesus would be ready to lead her beside the valley's still waters in future "garden" explorations. The dark valley is the place where Jesus brings His light and prepares a fantastic feast of good things, to sustain the grieving traveller as they travel *through* to the other side.

Holy Spirit tends to bring each session to a natural end, often marked by the explorer opening their eyes for the first time since the beginning of their journey; a good reason for the facilitator to keep their eyes open. Most explorers feel remarkably peaceful at this point. This is a good place for them to start their healing journey, for usually this is just the start of something much bigger to come. Often, all the explorer simply needed was that large spiritual space in which to find shelter and sustenance, before returning to the fray; feeling stronger and with the beginnings of answers. God does occasionally heal everything all in one go, but He loves journeying with us. So do encourage explorers to keep on experimenting with their garden. God is the healer and imagining being with Him activates encounter, reminiscent of the woman's healing when she 'touched the edge of His cloak' (Matthew 9:20); close encounters in *The Garden* will bring healing.

The walled garden as a ministry tool:
The spiritual walled garden is explored earlier in chapter 5 and is based on the 4th chapter of Song of Songs. It's a good tool to use for both groups and individuals, in private and confidential settings. It's helpful to have a photograph of the walled garden, for people to focus on.

The facilitator starts by inviting Holy Spirit to lead and may then read aloud Song of Songs 4:12-5:1. After that, it is explained to the person or group that they are about to enter the walled garden of their own hearts and that the door is open. Not only have we, as Christians, already opened the door to *The Garden* of our hearts to the Lord, but the cross tore the veil to the Holy of Holies and opened the door to *The Garden* of God's heart; John saw 'a door standing open in Heaven' (Revelation 4:1) and God longs for us to enter deeper into Him.

Then, the explorers are given a good twenty or thirty minutes to enter *The Gardens* of their hearts and experience anything the Lord has prepared for them there. The facilitator remains actively listening to Holy Spirit and may interject at given moments to ask: "What has God planted in *The Garden* of your heart?" or "Where is Jesus in your garden?" or "What is He saying?" A facilitator's job usually involves a certain amount of hand holding, while being careful to allow explorers freedom of experience and expression. God meets every individual on their own terms and only He knows best exactly where they are.

The explorers are encouraged to write down what they see and hear, either as they go along or at the end. Confidential sharing afterwards helps to consolidate everybody's experiences. There is often much excitement as a result of these forays, which can be spiritually life changing.

Using *The Garden* of a person's heart as an activation:
Asking anybody to imagine their heart as a garden can be a helpful device for creating encounter with the Lord, but also for establishing if there is anything in an explorer's life that may be inhibiting them from deepening their intimacy with God. God is speaking all the time and *The Garden* provides space to hear what He is saying. His Word is a very powerful and healing instrument, especially as He tailors what He says specifically to each person seeking His face. Because the Word of the Lord does not return empty, when God Himself speaks in an explorer's ear, seismic change begins to occur and something good is always destined to happen.

The activation for entering the ten-minute garden is on page 42 and this can be adapted for small groups or anybody receiving one-to-one ministry, either as a brief intervention to test the waters or as a much more leisurely endeavour. Most people are not only surprised at how easy it is to enter *The Garden* of their heart, but pleasantly surprised at what they find there. And most explorers will experience something of interest, even if it veers from what the facilitator might have expected. People are creative and God delights to work within whatever framework we offer Him. It's good to see any difficulties to entering *The Garden* as opportunities for God's intervention. Then the facilitator can work with what the explorer has in their hand; because that is exactly what God works with.

***The Garden* and the traumas of war:**
As far as I'm aware, *The Garden* as a healing tool for those with post-traumatic-stress disorder (PTSD) is as yet unchartered. But, it wouldn't surprise me if great and gentle healing could be achieved by PTSD sufferers accessing *The Garden* of their hearts, as long as their spirits and imaginations are surrendered to God.

My mother tells a story of my God Father, the late artist Albert Herbert, who was particularly known for his religious paintings. In the Second World War, he was marching with the invading army through the Normandy countryside on the way to Germany. They carried grenades and had to shelter in various places, even in graves for protection. One night, they found themselves in a village and took fright when they heard enemy voices across the other side of water, where there was also a stream. They became as quiet as church mice and laid low. As daylight approached, the voices moved off and Albert's small squad waited to be sure that they were quite safe, before emerging to find themselves in a large and exquisite garden revealed by the morning sun. In wonder, they walked around and explored the grounds. Albert said it felt like Heaven, it was so achingly beautiful. Years later, when Albert was Head of Painting at the Birmingham School of Art, he took his students on a trip to Monet's Water Garden at Giverny and realised that it was the very same garden from all those years ago!

So a young and upcoming artist, in the middle of a war, found himself in the peace and beauty of a garden, designed by an artist who was the master of colour and light and made famous by his many renditions of *Water Lilies*. At a time of great extremis, the water garden provided still waters for Albert to walk by and large areas of grass and trees in which he could find tranquillity. Similarly, *The Garden* woos us 'from the jaws of distress, to a spacious place free from restriction' (Job 36.16). God is the healer and His garden is a place of healing.

Resistance to entering *The Garden*:
Not everybody finds it easy to enter *The Garden*. Earthly circumstances can crowd in and drown out the heavenly. There are likely many reasons for such difficulties. But experiencing snags just means that the facilitator needs to be a bit more proactive in assisting access. Here are five examples of problematic garden entry that I have experienced as a facilitator, when leading various explorers:

1. ***Inexperience of life in Christ:*** When someone is very new to the faith, the old nature can interfere with the progress of the new identity's expansion. It takes time to put away the old and learn how to embrace the new. While a new Christian may have absolute certainty of the living God, they may have little or no experience of what it is to build a relationship with Him. I asked one lady—we'll call her Breda—if she could enter the walled garden through the door. Although God's door is always open, I had a clear picture in my mind of a closed door to Breda's walled garden and followed Holy Spirit in this vein. However, Breda wasn't even able to identify the door, because in her mind's eye everything was pitch black. I was able to reassure her that Psalm 139:11-12 tells us that, no matter how dark it feels, it's never dark for God; even 'darkness is as light to' Him. I asked her to imagine Jesus beside her and to put out her hand, to hold His. Then she was encouraged to feel for the handle of the door, turn it and enter. This she was able to do; the door opened and she was in.

2. ***Grief:*** Breda was also in the very early stages of grief, after the death of her husband. Unsurprisingly, the darkness she was experiencing was a mirror of her feelings of despair and loneliness at that time. On that first occasion, while she did finally manage to enter *The Garden*, everything remained black there. So I was able to tell her that Psalm 139:10 confirms that the Lord will always hold our hand and guide us through, no matter what the circumstances. Although not much more

progress was made that day, in later sessions *The Garden* of her heart did lighten up to reveal fields on a hill looking down over a valley and she was able to identify Jesus clearly standing with His back to her. Initially, she was able to approach Him and hold His hand. Eventually she stood before Him and heard Him speak to her. This all felt very gentle, but in fact was a ground-breaking moment; even little lambs know their Shepherd's voice and everything changes when they hear Him speak directly to them.

3. **Poor self esteem**: One lady—we'll call her Gilly—did manage to get into *The Garden* quite easily at her first attempt, but then found it difficult to repeat the experience. Gilly struggles with poor self esteem and felt frustrated with herself, when later attempts to enter *The Garden* seemed to come to nothing. Poor self esteem is frequently associated with lack of confidence, which can hijack the will to persevere. What's more is that low esteem commonly involves negative responses to oneself, involving unconstructive self criticism and generally thinking badly about oneself. *The Garden* in itself is a great place to learn to build confidence and self esteem, with God's abundant positivity and acceptance. But if a potential explorer can't get into *The Garden* in the first place, here are a few important keys to help unlock the door:

- Advise the explorer to set a guard over their mouth (Psalm 141:3) and speak only good over themself. Inform them that all positives come from God and all negatives are from the enemy. Recommend Don Gossett's (1976) book *What You Say Is What You Get!*
- Remind them that they were chosen in God, before the creation of the world, and that Jesus carried off all their negatives by dying on the cross. He sees us as the Groom sees the Bride in Song of Songs; we are always beautiful in His eyes. Graham Cooke (2015) tells the story of a dream, in which the Lord made it painfully clear to him that he had been taking back all the stuff, such as anxiety and depression, for which Jesus had died on the cross. So, encourage the explorer to give back to Jesus any stuff that they too may have taken back off the cross.
- Ask them to keep persevering, because, as Romans 5:3-5 says, difficulty 'produces perseverance; perseverance, character; and

character, hope. And hope does not put us to shame, because God's love has been poured out into our hearts through the Holy Spirit, who has been given to us.' Encourage them not to give up, because the rewards are huge. *The Garden* is a place where Jesus grows a person's true identity and it's all good.

- Encourage them to do a Freedom in Christ course (see pages 117-118 for details), which is a great foundation for the children of God. When a person knows who they really are in Christ, then they can do all things.

4. **Severe illness***:* The problem with being seriously ill is that physical symptoms can push themselves to the fore, knocking everything else sideways. One man—we'll call him Tim—had been very ill for a couple of months and, although his faith was strong, he found despair creeping in with the sheer persistence of his symptoms. I suggested that he enter *The Garden* as a way to get re-centred. Again I had a picture of a closed door to the walled garden. Tim couldn't even go near the door, let alone open it, and desperation began to creep in, freezing him to the spot. So I told him to imagine Jesus holding his hand. Then I explained to Tim that Jesus would open the door for him and take them both inside. Once within, I asked Tim if he could see anything. He couldn't, but it soon became apparent to both of us that Jesus was carrying Tim on His shoulder, as a sleeping newborn. What a wonderful picture of total rest, trust and sonship, with Jesus as the loving parent; patiently and lovingly seeing Tim through the hard yards. This was exactly where Tim needed to be at that point in his healing journey and he was able to relax, knowing that Jesus had it all in hand. I'm glad to report that Tim's health improved exponentially over the following months.

5. **Spiritual "slime":** *The Garden* is a multidimensional spiritual place in which to encounter God, but the enemy can put a spanner in the works with his own dark spiritual substance. This is why it is so important to surrender one's all to God, before entering *The Garden*. Amongst other things, such "slime" can result from:

- **Sin.** Sin occurs when a person, knowingly or unknowingly, goes their own way instead of God's. *The Garden* is a great place to deal with our sin. Jesus is so very gentle and loving and He knows how to train us to walk in His straight path. He makes confession fun. He once appeared to me in my mind's eye as a goal keeper and challenged me to kick the footballs of my sin into the net. Not one "sinball" got through; Jesus would catch them or stop them with His foot and explode every single one. My sin was unable to score me any points, because Jesus is too big and too good to let anything get passed Him. It was an extraordinarily freeing experience. Jesus is such a kind teacher and His lessons are always filled with joy.

As already expressed on page 46, I wonder now if my past swearing habit was the reason for satan[ii] appearing in my garden in the early days of going there. I saw him as a shadowy character standing at a distance, shouting awful insults at both me and Jesus; a sign of how outraged he was at my deepening intimacy with the Lord. But gradually, as I persevered with *The Garden*, satan[ii] disappeared. For all his bluster he has nothing on us, because all our negative stuff was nailed to the cross and that is where it needs to stay.

A lady—we'll call her Carol—entering *The Garden* in some group work I was leading, also saw a scary figure in her "garden". However, this figure was confined in its own walled garden, within a much bigger garden, and Carol was able to find still waters and green pastures elsewhere. My advice to her was not to focus on the dark figure but on the light, which she felt she had already been able to do. Cal Pierce, Director of Healing Rooms Ministries, frequently says that we embrace who we face. We face Jesus, because He fights our battles. In contrast, facing the enemy becomes a distraction and saps our faith. Our job is to get as close as we can to the Lord, so that the enemy has no access point. I encouraged Carol to return to her "garden" as often as she can, to give herself space for further tailored healing with the Lord. He will fight her battles. He will see to it that the dark figure is dealt with, as Carol makes progress in her "garden".

- **Unresolved physical or mental trauma from the past**. Undealt-with trauma gives access to the enemy, who likes to prod at it and make it fester. With regard to past trauma, it's good to seek help from trusted healing ministries, in which a person can be guided through additional healing processes. Healing Rooms are a good first port of call, as most teams have had training in inner healing and the ministry is free of charge. The Healing Rooms websites will help you find a Healing Room nearby. For Healing Rooms and other recommended ministries, see page 117. There is a prayer for breaking off fear, shock and trauma on page 109.

- **Unforgiveness.** As with undealt-with trauma, unforgiveness creates an access point for enemy invasion; see Matthew 18:21-35 in which unforgiveness gives the right to the enemy to imprison and torture the unforgiving person. The saying goes that unforgiveness is like drinking poison and hoping the other person dies. Unresolved bitterness has a habit of sapping joy, hope and faith and the burden of it can make life itself feel unbearable. Forgiving the other person might stick in the injured party's throat to begin with, but it's a process of being obedient in word and action in order to reap the rewards, which are enormous. Forgiveness is actually a lifestyle based on what Jesus has done on the cross. Because He has let us off scot free, we are duty bound to forgive and bear with others. Besides, there is only one judge and it's not us. There is a prayer of forgiveness on page 110.

- **Being cursed or having had association with some kind of witchcraft in the past.** Any previous contact with powers and forces that are not of God need to be renounced and replaced with God's love and promises (see page 139 for fifteen promises of God). The Seeker's prayer on page 16 is a good place to start.

    The enemy will try to hide his tactics behind seemingly honourable fronts. An example of this is Freemasonry, in which would-be members are compelled to make hundreds of oaths against themselves and their families. Such curses are not just a bit of fun, but create spiritual minefields for unsuspecting partakers. In the same vein, apparently harmless entities, such as horoscopes, palm reading and even *Harry Potter*, have questionable origins because they honour the channelling of anonymous power. Ouija boards are common fascinations for children, especially when they have no or little concept of the battle between dark and light. Any kind of dabbling needs confession, followed by the divine exchange; in which all the dark stuff is thrown down at the foot of the cross and replaced by all God's forgiveness, promises and protection.

Other religions can bring seemingly helpful practices into mainstream life, such as acupuncture and yoga. We each have to enquire of the Lord as to whether He thinks it safe for us to undergo this kind of treatment. There are many other examples of enemy influences. George Otis Junior (1997) makes it clear that dark spiritual substance clings to memes, i.e. those elements of cultural systems which are passed from one individual to another, across generations. Consequently, we proceed with caution: 'as shrewd as snakes and as innocent as doves' (Matthew 10:16). For a prayer breaking off enemy assignments, see page 114.

The Garden in intercession:

Intercession is a process through which spirit-led prayer is released into situations, to effect change for the good. Intercession bridges earthly gaps with heavenly structure, to make a way through where no way appears likely or possible. *The Garden* can provide part of this heavenly structure.

Mature intercessors move in spiritual gifts. They utilise their surrendered spiritual senses and imaginations for God's purposes; receiving pictures, words and scriptures, which inform them how to pray. God's sheep know His voice and intercessors are trained to receive and handle heavenly intelligence, relating to the matter in hand. This "intel" comes as revealed knowledge, inklings of God's thinking, and such insight can be very helpful in advancing the Kingdom's victory in difficult situations. This process can be extended into *The Garden* of a subject's heart and can be beneficial in accessing the wisdom, knowledge, understanding, discernment and counsel of Isaiah 11:2, in order to give direction to God's flow. It's not about gate-crashing or prying; it's a sensitive enquiry, with Godly guidance, in order to achieve rescue.

Compassion is vital for success; indeed, it forms part of the heavenly structure that bridges the gap between the earthly problem and the heavenly solution. On the one hand, an intercessor steps out of their comfort zone to come alongside an individual in their pain. On the other hand, they are constantly connected to the heart of God in the situation. Compassion is like rope used to save someone from drowning, with the intercessor connected both to the earthly issue as well as to the security of God's grip. This way, they don't get in over their heads and find themselves drowning in grief. God's compassion is always full of hope and comes to give life, as affirmed by Psalm 119:77.

The biggest advantage of *The Garden* in intercession is the depth of compassion it engenders in those praying. When an intercessor prayerfully imagines themself in *The Garden* of another's heart, they may get "on-the-ground intel" regarding the individual's perspective by way of experiencing sensations, emotions and insight that inform them more immediately about the circumstances at hand. This Heaven-supplied knowledge brings insight, understanding and empathy which opens 'a door of hope' (Hosea 2:15) from the valley of distress. In a sense, the intercessor is making a connection directly from God's heart to the subject's heart; bringing Heaven down to Earth.

I have used *The Garden* occasionally in intercession. A recent experience occurred during a group intercession meeting, as we prayed for a Christian girl we'll call Helen. She struggles with anorexia and is cared for in a specialist health institution. As I prayed, I found myself meditating on the joy I have in *The Garden* of my own heart, especially when building sand castles with Jesus on the beach there. I wondered how Helen could discover similar joy, as a form of respite from the desolation of a life full of the kind of constraints anorexia imposes. In my mind's eye, I tried to imagine the beach that might be there in *The Garden* of Helen's heart. Rather surprisingly, I found myself in a submarine under the sea, as though from Helen's perspective. Only the periscope was above the waves, observing the beach from a distance.

The impressions were multifactorial. The cramped space of the "sub" seemed to correlate to Helen's mental and physical confinement. Submarines are generally military vessels and I wondered what Helen was trying to protect herself from. My own imaginations of swimming in the sea of glass tell me that the children of God can breathe under water, yet Helen was encapsulated in this submarine. And instead of playing in the sand, Helen was observing from a distance; something was stopping her from taking pleasure in being closer to Jesus. Such "garden" experiences have helped us to pray into the battle lines, so far, on Helen's behalf. Determined intercession continues to secure the freedom, for which Christ has set Helen free, as promised in Galatians 5:1.

Confidentiality and intercession walk hand in hand and God trusts us with that responsibility, when we surrender to Him. If I do get a nudge from Holy Spirit to seek heavenly "intel" regarding someone's spiritual garden, it is always after submitting everything within myself to the Lord. This way, intentions and outcomes are as pure as possible. Of course, the person may never know I've prayed for them in such a way, but God knows; He calls us to follow Him, rather than going our own way. Christians, especially intercessors, do well to follow Moses' approach in Exodus 33:15 and not go anywhere without the Lord's leading and presence.

If the person in need is not a Christian, *The Garden* of their hearts is not yet inhabited by the presence of God. However, God saw *The Garden* of their heart before they were even born (Ecclesiastes 3:11, Ephesians 1:4), and He installed spiritual soil in them when He wove them together in their mother's womb. So, even if they don't yet know they have a spirit, they still have some kind of garden in their heart.

Nevertheless, an intercessor would have to be very confident of God's presence and guidance to set foot in such a garden. I have done it once for a girl I've never met, whom I'll call Nelly. She lived abroad and was suffering with breast cancer. God really placed Nelly on my heart and I carried a burden of intercession for her. I asked the Lord how I should pray for her and began imagining the place where she lived. Once my imagination was activated, before I realised it, I was wandering in *The Garden* of Nelly's heart. My impression of her garden was that it was wild and disorganised. I felt no danger to myself, but only aware of the many barriers in the internal and external spaces that I saw in my mind's eye. Walls of outdoor thorn bushes abounded and there was a garden-house with a mishmash of beams, from ceiling to floor, prohibiting any movement inside. I just prayed whatever I felt Holy Spirit was telling me and experienced huge amounts of compassion for this person, as I did so. I'm glad to say that Nelly recovered.

'I know' by the late Sarah McCrum

Chapter 10

Prayers for Inner Healing

'It is for freedom that Christ has set us free.'
(Galatians 5:1)

It may be that previous chapters have highlighted areas in your life that need healing. Physical, emotional and relational problems can develop as a result of dark spiritual forces finding a variety of entry points into our lives and messing us up as a result. But, as a child of God, you have the authority and the power to boot out such dark matter and replace it with heavenly healing, on the proviso that you don't stop any medication or treatment without a doctor validating your healing; generally speaking, health professionals are the salt of the earth and do a crucial job.

All the prayers in this chapter are designed to be spoken aloud. 'It is with your mouth that you profess your faith and are saved' (Romans 10:10); as explained on page 61, when surrendered to God, the spoken word changes atmospheres. The prayers are designed to be a good starting point, before considering any need for further ministry. A simple prayer and declaration, in the presence of Holy Spirit, may be all it takes to set you free. If not, there is a list of helpful healing ministries at the end of this chapter on pages 117-118.

Dealing with unhealthy soul ties:

It's good to bond with the people we love; family members, spouses and friends. Bonds entail commitment, which connects us together and involves mutual sharing. But it's vital to be aware that heredity in families, sexual intercourse in a physical relationship and making an oath in a relationship/friendship are not just familial or social bonds, but also spiritual. This means that such bonds involve the sharing of "spiritual substance".

One type of unhealthy soul tie is the bond which hasn't been broken at the end of a relationship, through death, divorce or separation. Unless they are dealt with, the spiritual bonds formed with someone we formerly loved can become more like fetters that stop us moving on with our lives.

However, grief is a process and different for everybody; so it's important to be in the right place before breaking a soul tie, especially if the other person has died. Nevertheless, hanging on for years to a person who has died can attract dark forces, which will readily tug on bonds that should no longer be active. This can lead to a scenario in which an individual so yearns for the dead person that they start to experience paranormal activity. They may truly believe that they can see and communicate with their lost loved one, when in actual fact the enemy has implanted a shadowy imposter. With the loss of a child—through cot death, miscarriage or abortion—unbroken soul ties to the lost infant can often manifest as physical symptoms, such as migraine and infertility.

All penetrative sexual encounters generate soul ties, whether wanted or not, including those in rape and abusive relationships. Breaking soul ties is an important first step on the road to healing from sexual trauma and into the freedom of living your own life, unencumbered by someone else's spiritual substance. It's good to break every soul tie ever made this way, one by one.

Another kind of unhealthy soul tie is created by making an "unholy vow" in relationship to another person. This is a declaration that is thought or spoken by one individual in relation to another, which may unwittingly go against God's divine will and purpose, thereby causing unintended damage to both parties. So, for example, should a character declare to God that they would gladly give their life in exchange for the other person becoming a Christian, they have formed a death bond which makes the other individual's "salvation" dependent upon the first's demise. No matter how kind and giving this vow might seem, only Jesus saves and so it goes against the finished work of the cross. The result is the formation of an unseen manacle of dark influence between the two people concerned, even if the other character has no idea about such a vow.

Prayer to break off soul ties from a loved one who has died:

(Say this aloud)

Dear Lord God, I thank You that you put .... (name) in my life and for all they were to me and for all the good they brought me. I am sorry if I ever hurt them and forgive them if they ever hurt me. Thank You that I can enjoy beautiful memories of them and thank You that I do not need to worry about them, because they are now in Your loving arms. You chose them in You before the creation of the world and set eternity in their heart. I trust them to Your heavenly care and completely hand them over to You.

I now step away, breaking the soul ties between me and .... (name)

(Clap, as a sign that the soul tie is broken)

Now, by way of your divine exchange, fill me with your perfect love, Your everlasting life and Your supernatural strength.

(Pause to allow God's spiritual infilling of your soul)

I now step into and embrace my new life on Earth, in and with You. I declare that I can do all things through Christ, who strengthens me and that Your plan for my life is full of hope and goodness, to prosper me and not to harm me. I welcome life in You, which promises life in all its fullness.

Amen.

Prayer to break off soul ties from a sexual partner with whom a relationship has ended:

(Say this aloud)

Dear Lord God, I thank You for .... (name) and for all the good things they brought into my life. I am sorry for anything I have done to hurt them and I forgive them for any wrong doing towards me. I release both myself and them into the freedom of my forgiveness.

I give them back any residual spiritual substance that they may have deliberately or inadvertently left in me and take back any of my spiritual substance that I may have freely or involuntarily deposited in them.

(Pause and breathe deeply, to allow this to happen)

I now declare that we are no longer one body, but two separate people and that we are both free to live the lives that you have set before us.

(Clap at this point, as a sign of the soul tie breaking)

Now, by way of your divine exchange, fill me with your perfect love, Your everlasting life and Your supernatural strength.

(Pause and breathe deeply, to allow God's spiritual infilling of your soul)

I now step into and embrace my new life in and with You. I declare that I can do all things through Christ, who strengthens me and that Your plan for my life is full of hope and goodness, to prosper me and not to harm me. I welcome life in You, which promises life in all its fullness.

Amen.

Prayer to break off soul ties, formed by making an unholy vow:
(Say this aloud)

Dear Lord God, I am sorry that I made a vow that flouted your Word and Your will for my life and for the life of............. (name). Please forgive me, even if I didn't mean to do it or intend any harm by it. I now break this vow, as though it had never been said or thought.

(Clap at this point, as a sign of the soul tie breaking. Breathe deeply to let the truth of this declaration sink in)

I now declare that we are both free from the bondage of that vow, to live the lives that You have set before us.

By way of Your divine exchange, I declare your blessings upon both of our lives, that both of us may come to know You ever more clearly, to love You ever more dearly and to follow You ever more nearly, from this day forward.

Amen.

Dealing with fear, shock and trauma:

If not dealt with, any experience involving fear, shock and trauma can leave its mark on one's body, soul and spirit. Before you pray, it's good to ask God to reveal the occurrences in your life that appear to be the root cause(s) of your current issue(s). When you allow Holy Spirit to do this, you may be surprised by what crops up. Don't be dismayed, but be faithful and just run with it. When you hand it all over to God and receive the divine exchange in return, miracles can happen.

Prayer to break off fear, shock and trauma:
(Say this aloud)

Dear Lord God, I thank you for .... (take your time as you name all the episodes in your life that have involved fear, shock and trauma of any kind), because You work good in all things for those that love You and I am learning to love You.

I break off all fear, shock and trauma that entered into my body, soul and spirit, as a result of these events, and send them to the foot of the cross; where they will stay and not come back or be taken back by me.

(Clap your hands as a sign that the fear, shock and trauma have left your body, soul and spirit)

I declare that I am now free from fear, shock and trauma!

(Breathe deeply as the truth of this declaration sinks in)

Now, by way of your divine exchange, I receive Your perfect love, which drives out fear.

(Take long slow breaths for a minute or two, as a sign that you are receiving God's love, into your body, soul and spirit)

And I receive Your perfect peace, that passes all understanding; so I relinquish my right to understand, so that I no longer need to make sense of what is happening.

(Take long slow breaths for a minute or two, as a sign that you are receiving God's peace, into your body, soul and spirit)

And I receive Your heavenly healing, which is my rightful inheritance, because of what You did on the cross for me.

(Take long slow breaths for a minute or two, as a sign that you are receiving God's healing into your body, soul and spirit)

Thank You Lord Jesus for what you have done with my past, for what you are doing in my present and for all the good things

You have planned for my future. I believe and trust in You and step into the life You have set before me with confidence, purpose and optimism.

Amen.

Dealing with unforgiveness:

Bill Johnson and Kris Valloton (2006) explain clearly why we must forgive others. They refer to Matthew 18:21-35 in which the unforgiving servant is put in gaol to be tormented:

> *'Unforgiveness puts us in prison. If we fail to understand how big our debt of sin was to God and what it meant for Him to forgive it, we can fall into the trap of judging the much smaller wrongs of those around us. As we can see from the story, we are only hurting ourselves when we do that. God insists that His people forgive each other, and He's not above using the devil as a pawn to help us do it.'*

This makes it clear that forgiveness is vital, if we are to experience freedom from the kind of torture to which the unforgiving servant made himself subject. For most people, forgiveness is a process. It can begin with saying words of forgiveness we don't yet mean, but perseverance will 'finish its work' (James 1:4) and bring us into line with the One who paid the price to forgive us all. In the end, it is ourselves we are setting free, through a doorway of forgiveness.

A prayer of forgiveness:
(Say this aloud)

Dear Lord God, I want to forgive .... (name/s) against whom I have been bearing a grudge, even if my feelings don't yet feel ready. I know that there is no condemnation in Christ. I believe and trust that You always give me the strength to do all things, including the strength to forgive.

I no longer want to be a prisoner of unforgiveness and I no longer want to be tortured by its effects. I forgive .... (name/s) for the suffering I feel I have endured at their hands and I release them into the freedom of my forgiveness. I will keep forgiving them, until I feel the process of forgiveness is complete.

I also forgive myself for any kind of self blame. I will keep forgiving myself, until I know that I am free.

And I forgive You, my God, for any blame I have placed on You. I will keep forgiving You, until I know that I am free.

I send all my past unforgiveness to the foot of the cross and I declare that I will not take it back. Instead, by way of Your divine exchange, I receive Your love, healing and freedom. I declare that You have made me free to live the life You have set before me; a life in which I will bless my enemies, endure persecution and answer kindly those who slander me. I believe that You work good in all things, no matter what life brings, and I declare that I am more than a conqueror through You, who loves me.

Thank You Lord!

Amen.

Dealing with the occult:

The seeker's prayer on page 16 includes a brief renunciation of any previous involvement in the occult, e.g. ouija boards, tarot cards, horoscopes, fortune telling and even reading/watching *Harry Potter*. For those who have actively been involved in a witch's coven in the past, I suggest you contact Restoring The Foundations or CHUK (details on page 118) for help from a dedicated ministry in this area. For those who have had previous direct or indirect involvement with Freemasonry, Otto Bixler's (2016) book *It Isn't Free And It Isn't Masonry* is an excellent doorway to release from Freemasonry's unseen curses for ex-masons, their families and descendants.

Dealing with curses, hexes, negative assignments and negative words made against you:

Spotting enemy action:
It's easy to spot negative words when they are said aloud in your presence, but curses, hexes and negative assignments against you can be very covert. Indeed, you may have no idea who is trying to mess you up through such insidious means. What you might notice is a spate of unexpected illnesses and unfortunate accidents or incidents, which impede your life journey. Sometimes, paranormal activity can take place around you or physical evidence of hexes can appear in your path. Attack can come through other people, especially if they are beholden to occultic activities. If such characters are in positions of power and importance, you will notice that false accusations, lies, intimidation and control feature strongly in their dealings with you. This is because the enemy is 'a liar and the father of lies' (John 8:44). But we wear God's 'belt of truth' (Ephesians 6:14) and the book of Revelation makes it clear that God's victory is already won.

However, if you experience any of the things mentioned above, be encouraged because you must be doing something right. We are in a battle that has been raging since satan[ii] was thrown out of Heaven (see Luke 10:18) and we simply have to remember that we are on the winning side. This means that we can be confident in dealing with such attack. Below are a few helpful heavenly tools for the battle.

1. Don't be afraid:
I heard Bill Johnson say once, 'We all get "slimed"'. Indeed, the deeper we go into God, the less covert the enemy seems to become. Significantly for us, we have no need to be afraid of this foe, because God's perfect love for us drives out fear. Furthermore, our ability to quench the enemy's flaming arrows is certain and rests on knowing that Jesus lives within us. Carrying His presence within us enables us to do all things through Him, including quashing enemy action. This is because all power and authority in all Heaven and Earth has been given to Jesus (Matthew 28:18), the one who is in you and who 'is greater than the one who is in the world' (1 John 4:4). With all this in mind, we confidently approach all attack from a position of victory.

2. Face God:
One of the crucial ways of stepping into God's victory is to look to Him and not to focus on what the enemy is doing. In the Healing Rooms Ministries training video, Cal Pierce (2014) advises:

> *'Don't face your enemy, because what you face is what you embrace. Draw close to God and face Him. Resist the enemy and he will flee from you... God is light. The closer we come to God, the more illuminated we are and the more resistance we have against the enemy. Our light will overcome the devil's darkness. We have to come to that place where we have a full-time God and then we won't need a devil'.*

Beni Johnson (2013) compares our battle to the coded "plays" (plans of attack) in American football. If a team's players were to listen to the plays of the opponents' team, they would lose focus on their own team strategy. Rather, we listen to the "plays" coming from God, the captain of our lives. That way, we don't get distracted by what the enemy is trying to do.

3. Put on your armour:
Additionally, it's good to daily put on the armour of God:

> *'Put on the full armour of God, so that you can take your stand against the devil's schemes. For our struggle is not against flesh and blood, but against the rulers, against the authorities, against the powers of this dark world and against the spiritual forces of evil in the heavenly realms. Therefore put on the full armour of God, so that when the day of evil comes, you may be able to stand your ground, and after you have done everything, to stand. Stand firm then, with the belt of truth buckled around your waist, with the breastplate of righteousness in place, and with your feet fitted with the readiness that comes from the gospel of peace. In addition to all this, take up the shield of faith, with which you can extinguish all the flaming arrows of the evil one. Take the helmet of salvation and the sword of the Spirit, which is the word of God. And pray in the Spirit on all occasions with all kinds of prayers and requests. With this in mind, be alert and always keep on praying for all the Lord's people.'*
> (Ephesians 6:10-18)

Meditate on this scripture; think deeply about what each of the elements represents in Christ and which part of you is being protected. Then, ask

Jesus to dress you in His heavenly armour (see my own experience of this in the middle of page 44). When Jesus dresses you, the armour doesn't fall off.

4. Bless those who curse you:
Furthermore, as children of God, 'when we are cursed, we bless' (1 Corinthians 4:12). Why? Because our struggle is not against people of any kind. Every human being has been chosen in God, before the creation of the world, whether or not they have yet to choose Him back. Rather, our fight is against supernatural powers. Therefore, we come out in the opposite spirit, blessing those who curse us; a wonderfully positive and powerful heavenly weapon. Blessing a person causes confusion in the supernatural enemy's camp, thereby quenching the foe's flaming arrows.

> ***A healing prayer breaking off enemy assignments,***
> ***by Rev Ray Scorey:***
> (Say this aloud)
>
> *In the name of the Father, the Son and the Holy Spirit, I take authority given to me and speak against every spirit of infirmity, assignment, word, hex, curse, spell, negative prayer, hindrance, disqualification or false teaching that has had any kind of negative effect on me. I command each and every one of them to go to that place that Jesus has prepared for such things, breaking every single one off me now. I claim the power of the cross over me.*
>
> *Now Lord, please release Your healing, love, grace, power, strength, confidence and a sense of wellbeing and personal worth. I call my immune system to identify the source of this attack and get rid of it now. I counter all my distress with the positiveness of God and throw into confusion and depression the work of the enemy. By Jesus' stripes I am healed!*
>
> *Above all this, I choose to trust in You Lord, in Your cross, in the power of Your shed blood and resurrection power. Heaven's angels attend me now. I speak authority over my spirit, with the authority You have given me, for it is my position in God that matters and not my earthly condition. God's Word says, those who wait upon the Lord will renew their strength. So I will rise*

up in joyful praise and adoration, because in all things God works for the good of those that love Him.

I now rest in You, as I seek more of you Lord. I'm hungry for you, more than I am fearful. Thank You for Your restoring grace. Thank You so much for Your love, joy and peace falling upon me now. The glory of Your presence touches me, so be blessed with my praise as I glory in Your embrace and as Your presence now fills this room.

Amen.

How to keep your healing

This is advice Norfolk Healing Rooms hand out to guests.

Know who you are in Christ: Did you know that you were chosen in Christ before the creation of the world (Ephesians 1:4)? Even when you didn't know Jesus, He has always been on your side (Romans 5:8). Once born again, you are a royal child of the Most High God and He says He will never leave you or forsake you (Hebrews 13:5); nothing can separate you from the love of God (Romans 8:31-39). He has a plan for your life, to give you a hope and a future (Jeremiah 29:11), so take heart and walk in confidence in your birthright.

Believe God's Word: When we understand and believe God's Word on healing, we can "stand on the Word" (the rock of our foundation) to bring mental, physical and spiritual healing. God's truth is that by Jesus' stripes we *were* healed (Isaiah 53:5); we haven't just been saved but healed too; past, present and future. When we get this truth under our belts, we align ourselves with Heaven and start to bring heavenly health into our bodies.

Declare God's truth and promises over yourself: As well as believing what God says about healing, it is important to speak His promises aloud over yourself, (see page 139 for fifteen promises of God). The power of the spoken word cannot be overemphasised. When the world was created, God called into being that which was not as though it were (Romans 4:17). Therefore, Spirit-filled Christians also have this same power and authority to declare God's word aloud for healing.

Avoid Negatives: All positives come from God, but all negatives come from the enemy, who seeks only to steal, kill and destroy (John 10:10). So be aware of avoiding all negatives, so that you don't let your words do the work of the enemy. This is what Paul means about taking every thought captive; despite the apparently numerous thoughts in your head, this really is possible and it gets easier with practise. When you identify a negative thought, boot it out and replace it with one of God's promises.

Give thanks in all circumstances: Because God works good in all things for those who love Him (Romans 8:28), acknowledging this through thanksgiving breaks agreement with the enemy and releases blessings, that neutralise enemy action. So it's good to thank God in and *for* ALL things, even if it's through gritted teeth to begin with. It's an act of obedience and a sacrifice of praise.

Know God's authority is over all: Sometimes it can be hard to ignore a doctor's diagnosis/prognosis when spoken over you by someone so revered. But once you know who you are in Christ, when you believe His promises and declare His truths over yourself, you will come to realise that His Word and His truth have more power even than that of a respected doctor. We thoroughly recommend that you watch *Destroying Cancer* by Cal Pierce (YouTube 2015).

Even if you haven't been given a cancer diagnosis, this "Kingdom thinking" approach helps to align your thinking with God's. Earthly facts are one thing, but Heavenly truth is quite another (2 Corinthians 4:18). If symptoms return, treat them like negative thoughts: tell them to go in the name of Jesus and speak God's promises over yourself instead. Resist the devil and he will flee (James 4:7).

Consider taking daily communion: We fully recommend taking communion on a daily basis. In this way, we remember that Christ not only died for our salvation, but for our healing and for life in all its fullness. His body is like a seed of healing and His life-giving blood waters the seed.

WHERE TO GET FURTHER HELP:

Healing Rooms Ministries: *www.healingrooms.com*
Healing Rooms Ministries is a global movement of healing, with Jesus at the core. It exists to see people healed, set free, and launched into their destiny by demonstrating the Kingdom of God right here, right now. Healing Rooms Ministries is founded on Jesus' commission in Mark 16 that believers, when armed with the Holy Spirit, have authority and power over any sickness or infirmity. There are hundreds of locations in sixty-eight countries. Visit the website to find a location near you.

***Healing Rooms England & Wales* (HREW):** *www.healingrooms.org.uk*
There are numerous Healing Rooms in the UK. They offer guests free, short, face-to-face-sessions—or via phone/Zoom—which are Spirit-led and Bible based, with trained teams of three who are gentle and loving. All sessions are backed up by a team of intercessors. More than one session may be required. Go to the website to find a Healing Room near you.

UK National Prayer Line: *03300 889 336*
The UK National Prayer Line is run by trained members of HREW, in association with UK's United Christian Broadcasters, and offers short, phone-call, prayer ministry. The prayer line runs Monday to Saturday, 10.30am-12.30pm (excluding Bank Holidays).

Healing Rooms Australia: *www.healingrooms.com.au*
Healing Rooms South Africa: *www.healingafrica.co.za*
Healing Rooms Singapore: *www.facebook.com/HealingRoomsSG*

Bethel Sozo:
Sozo means healed, saved, restored and protected. This inner healing ministry was initiated by Dawna De Silva at Bethel Church, Redding, California. It involves a two-hour session with a trained practitioner, lots of participant interaction and a process which restores the family—earthly and heavenly—through dealing with root issues. There is no charge for Sozo, but donations are gratefully accepted.
Bethel Sozo USA: *www.bethelsozo.com*
Bethel Sozo UK: *www.bethelsozo.org.uk*
Bethel Sozo Australia: *www.bethelsozoaustralia.com*
Bethel Sozo South Africa: *https://sozosouthafrica.co.za*
Bethel Sozo Singapore: *www.bethelsozo.com/singapore*

Freedom in Christ Course:
The Freedom in Christ Course is a ten-session discipleship MOT course, ideal for small groups, with flexible teaching sessions that reveal the truth of who we are in Christ and the reality of the spiritual battle. The final key is "stronghold-busting";

being transformed by the renewal of our mind by demolishing arguments set up against God. Go to the website to find a course near you.
Freedom in Christ USA: *www.ficm.org*
Freedom in Christ UK: *www.ficm.org.uk/discipleship-course*
Freedom in Christ Australia: *www.freedominchrist.org/country/australia*
Freedom in Christ South Africa: *www.freedominchrist.org/country/south-africa*

Heart Healing at Be.Prophetic: *www.beprophetic.net/services-1-1*
Christine Wren James runs "Heart Matters" healing courses online via Zoom from Australia. Course 1 teaches on: hidden vows; buried pain and its effect on the body; walls and false refuges; grief and loss; why we find it hard to trust; soul ties; forgiveness and walking through a wilderness time and befriending our trials. Course 2 teaches on: healing of memories; finding true identity; the effects of emotional autism; roots of rejection; co-dependency and trauma recovery (Australian price $150 AUD per person, per course*).

Restoring the Foundations (RTF)
RTF is an international organisation and offers a three-hour *Issue Focused Ministry* (UK price £150 per person*) and five three-hourly sessions of *Thorough Format Ministry* (UK price £750 per person*). Sessions involve in-depth inner healing for individuals or couples. RTF will deal with demonic oppression.
RTF International: *restoringthefoundations.org*
RTF UK: *www.restoringthefoundations.uk*
RTG South Africa: *www.facebook.com/RestoringTheFoundationsSa*
RTF Singapore: *www.restoringthefoundations.asia*

Christian Healing UK (CHUK): *www.christianhealinguk.org*
This UK website has a list of UK healing ministries, tailored to a wide variety of needs including ministries that deal with occultic oppression.

(2023 prices)*

If you do choose other ministries, ensure that they move in the love of God and practise the divine exchange, in which ministers always spiritually infill a person with all God's good stuff, after helping an individual to discard ungodly spiritual elements. The divine exchange is based on Luke 11:24-26, in which a 'house' (or person's spirit), swept clean of an impure spirit, is re-inhabited by even more evil spirits when they find the house clean, but empty. The establishment of the presence of God and all His gifts in a person's heart prevents such a scenario. This is what we interpret Matthew 16:19 to mean by binding and loosing. We bind the enemy and loose the heavenly.

APPENDIX 1

A Bible Full of Garden Imagery

Here is a selection of scriptures (in biblical order) that use references to gardens, vineyards, countryside, trees and fruits as metaphors and similes. They emphasise how important *The Garden* is to Father God.

Genesis:

'Now the Lord God had planted a garden in the east, in Eden; and there He put the man He had formed. The Lord God made all kinds of trees grow out of the ground - trees that were pleasing to the eye and good for food. In the middle of the garden were the tree of life and the tree of the knowledge of good and evil. A river watering the garden flowed from Eden... The Lord God took the man and put him in the Garden of Eden to work it and take care of it.' **(Genesis 2:8-10,15)**

Numbers:

'How beautiful are your tents, Jacob, your dwelling-places, Israel! Like valleys they spread out, like gardens beside a river, like aloes planted by the Lord, like cedars beside the waters.' **(Numbers 24:5-7)**

Deuteronomy:

'For the Lord your God is bringing you into a good land - a land with brooks, streams, and deep springs gushing out into the valleys and hills; a land with wheat and barley, vines and fig-trees, pomegranates, olive oil and honey; a land where bread will not be scarce and you will lack nothing.' **(Deuteronomy 8:7-9)**

1 Kings:

'For the entrance to the inner sanctuary he made doors out of olive wood that were one fifth of the width of the sanctuary. And on the two olive-wood doors he carved cherubim, palm trees and open flowers, and overlaid the cherubim and palm trees with hammered gold.' **(1 Kings 6:31-32)**

Psalms:

'Blessed is the one who does not walk in step with the wicked or stand in the way that sinners take or sit in the company of mockers, but whose delight is in the law of the Lord, and who meditates on His law day and night. That person is like a tree planted by streams of water, which yields its fruit in season and whose leaf does not wither - whatever they do prospers.' **(Psalm 1:1-3)**

'I am like an olive tree flourishing in the house of God; I trust in God's unfailing love for ever and ever.' **(Psalm 52:8)**

'The righteous will flourish like a palm tree, they will grow like a cedar of Lebanon; planted in the house of the Lord, they will flourish in the courts of God. They will still bear fruit in old age, they will stay fresh and green, proclaiming, "The Lord is upright; He is my Rock, and there is no wickedness in Him."' **(Psalm 92:12-15)**

Proverbs:

'[Wisdom] is a tree of life to those who take hold of her; those who hold her fast will be blessed.' **(Proverbs 3:18)**

'The fruit of the righteous is a tree of life, and the one who is wise saves lives.' **(Proverbs 11:30)**

'Hope deferred makes the heart sick, but a longing fulfilled is a tree of life.' **(Proverbs 13:12)**

'The soothing tongue is a tree of life, but a perverse tongue crushes the spirit.' **(Proverbs 15:4)**

'One who guards a fig tree will eat its fruit.' **(Proverbs 27:18)**

Song of Songs:

'She: My beloved is to me a cluster of henna blossoms from the vineyards of En Gedi.' **(Song of Songs 1:14)**

'She: I am a rose of Sharon, a lily of the valleys.
He: Like a lily among thorns is my darling among the young women
She: Like an apple tree among the trees of the forest is my beloved among the young men. I delight to sit in His shade, and His fruit is sweet to my taste.' **(Song of Songs 2:1-3)**

'He: See! The winter is past; the rains are over and gone.
Flowers appear on the earth; the season of singing has come,
The cooing of doves is heard in our land.
The fig-tree forms its early fruit; the blossoming vines spread their fragrance.' **(Song of Songs 2:11-13)**

'He: Catch for us the foxes, the little foxes that ruin the vineyards, our vineyards that are in bloom.' **(Song of Songs 2:15)**

'She: My beloved is mine and I am his; He browses among the lilies.' **(Song of Songs 2:16)**

'He: You are a garden locked up, my sister, my bride;
You are a spring enclosed, a sealed fountain.
Your plants are an orchard of pomegranates with choice fruits,
with henna and nard, nard and saffron,
Calamus and cinnamon, with every kind of incense tree,
with myrrh and aloes and all the finest spices.
You are a garden fountain,
a well of flowing water streaming down from Lebanon.
She: Awake, north wind, and come, south wind!

	Blow on my garden, that its fragrance may spread everywhere. Let my beloved come into His garden and taste its choice fruits.' **(Song of Songs 4:12-16)**
'He:	I have come into my garden, my sister, my bride; I have gathered my myrrh with my spice.' **(Song of Songs 5:1)**
'She:	He has gone down to His garden, to the beds of spices, to browse in the gardens and to gather lilies. I am my beloved's and my beloved is mine; He browses among the lilies.' **(Song of Songs 6:2-3)**
'He:	I went down to the grove of nut trees to look at the new growth in the valley, to see if the vines had budded or the pomegranates were in bloom.' **(Song of Songs 6:11)**
'He:	I said, "I will climb the palm tree; I will take hold of its fruit. May your breasts be like clusters of grapes on the vine, the fragrance of your breath like apples and your mouth like the best wine."' **(Song of Songs 7:8-9)**
'He:[1]	When I awakened you under the apple tree, as you were feasting upon me, I awakened your innermost being with the travail of birth.' **(Song of Songs 8:5, *The Passion Translation*, 2020)**
'He:	You who dwell in the gardens with friends in attendance, let me hear your voice!' **(Song of Song 8:13)**

Isaiah:

'The vineyard of the Lord Almighty is the nation of Israel, and the people of Judah are the vines He delighted in.' **(Isaiah 5:7)**

'A shoot will come up from the stump of Jesse; from his roots a Branch will bear fruit.' **(Isaiah 11:1)**

'In that day the Root of Jesse will stand as a banner for the peoples.'
(Isaiah 11:10)

'Sing about a fruitful vineyard; I, the Lord, watch over it; I water it continually.'
(Isaiah 27:2b-3a)

'In days to come Jacob will take root, Israel will bud and blossom and fill all the world with fruit.' **(Isaiah 27:6)**

'The lord will make Zion's deserts like Eden and her wastelands like the garden of the Lord.' **(Isaiah 51:3)**

'He grew up before Him like a tender shoot and like a root out of dry ground.'
(Isaiah 53:2)

---

[1] *The NIV translation assigns this verse to the Bride; The Passion Translation to the Bridegroom, which appears to make more sense.*

'"For my thoughts are not your thoughts, neither are your ways my ways" declares the Lord. As the heavens are higher than the earth, so are my ways higher than your ways and my thoughts than your thoughts. As the rain and the snow come down from heaven, and do not return to it without watering the earth and making it bud and flourish, so that it yields seeds for the sower and bread for the eater, so is my word that goes out from my mouth: it will not return to me empty, but will accomplish what I desire and achieve the purpose for which I sent it. You will go out in joy and be led forth in peace; the mountains and hills will burst into song before you, and all the trees of the field will clap their hands. Instead of the thornbush will grow the juniper, and instead of briers the myrtle will grow. This will be for the Lord's renown, for an everlasting sign, that will endure forever.' **(Isaiah 55:9-13)**

'The Lord will guide you always; He will satisfy your needs in a sun-scorched land and will strengthen your frame. You will be like a well-watered garden, like a spring whose waters never fail.' **(Isaiah 58:11)**

'For as the soil makes the young plant come up and a garden causes seeds to grow, so the Sovereign Lord will make righteousness and praise spring up before all nations.' **(Isaiah 61:11)**

Jeremiah:

'They will be like a tree planted by the water that sends out its roots by the stream. It does not fear when heat comes; its leaves are always green. It has no worries in a year of drought and never fails to bear fruit.' **(Jeremiah 17:8)**

'They will be like a well-watered garden.' **(Jeremiah 31:12)**

Hosea:

'I will be like the dew to Israel; he will blossom like a lily. Like a cedar of Lebanon he will send down his roots; his young shoots will grow. His splendour will be like an olive tree, his fragrance like a cedar of Lebanon. People will dwell again in his shade; they will flourish like the corn, they will blossom like the vine.' **(Hosea 14:5-7)**

Joel:

'Do not be afraid, you wild animals, for the pastures in the wilderness are becoming green. The trees are bearing their fruit; the fig-tree and the vine yield their riches.' **(Joel 2:22)**

Amos:

'"The days are coming", declares the Lord, "when the reaper will be overtaken by the ploughman and the planter by the one treading grapes. New wine will drip from the mountains and flow from all the hills, and I will bring my people Israel back from exile. They will rebuild the ruined cities and live in them. They will plant vineyards and drink their wine/ they will make gardens and eat their fruit. I will plant Israel in their own land, never again to be uprooted from the land I have given them."' **(Amos 9:13-15)**

Micah:

'Everyone will sit under their own vine and under their own fig-tree, and no one will make them afraid, for the Lord Almighty has spoken.' **(Micah 4:4)**

Habakkuk:

'Though the fig-tree does not bud and there are no grapes on the vines, though the olive crop fails and the fields produce no food, though there are no sheep in the sheepfold and no cattle in the stalls, yet I will rejoice in the Lord, I will be joyful in God my Saviour.' **(Habakkuk 3:17-18)**

Matthew:

'Make a tree good and its fruit will be good, or make a tree bad and its fruit will be bad, for a tree is recognised by its fruit.' **(Matthew 12:33)**

'A farmer went out to sow his seed. As he was scattering the seed, some fell along the path, and the birds came and ate it up. Some fell on rocky places, where it did not have much soil. It sprang up quickly, because the soil was shallow. But when the sun came up, the plants were scorched, and they withered because they had no root. Other seed fell among thorns, which grew up and choked the plants. Still other seed fell on good soil, where it produced a crop - a hundred, sixty or thirty times what was sown. Whoever has ears, let them hear.' **(Matthew 13:3-9)**

'What is the kingdom of God like: what shall I compare it to? It is like a mustard seed, which a man took and planted in his garden. It grew and became a tree and the birds perched in its branches.' **(Matthew 13:18-19)**

'For the Kingdom of Heaven is like a landowner who went out early in the morning to hire workers for His vineyard.' **(Matthew 20:1)**

Luke:

'No good tree bears bad fruit, nor does a bad tree bear good fruit. Each tree is recognised by its own fruit. People do not pick figs from thorn-bushes, or grapes from briers. A good man brings good things out of the good stored up in his heart, and an evil man brings evil things out of the evil stored up in his heart. For the mouth speaks what the heart is full of.' **(Luke 6:43-45)**

'Then the owner of the vineyard said, "What shall I do? I will send My Son, whom I love."' **(Luke 20:13)**

'He told them this parable: Look at the fig-tree and all the trees. When they sprout leaves, you can see for yourselves and know that summer is near. Even so, when you see these things happening, you know that the kingdom of God is near.' **(Luke 21:29-31)**

John:

'I am the true vine, and my Father is the gardener.' **(John 15:1)**

'I am the vine; you are the branches. If you remain in me and I in you, you will bear much fruit; apart from me you can do nothing.' **(John 15:5)**

Romans:

'If the root is holy, so are the branches. If some of the branches have been broken off, and you, though a wild olive shoot, have been grafted in among the others and now share in the nourishing sap from the olive root, do not consider yourself to be superior to those other branches. If you do, consider this; you do not support the root, but the root supports you.' **(Romans 11:16-17)**

Revelation:

'Whoever has ears, let them hear what the Spirit says to the churches. To the one who is victorious, I will give the right to eat from the tree of life, which is in the paradise of God.' **(Revelation 2:7)**

'Then the angel showed me the river of the water of life, as clear as crystal, flowing from the throne of God and of the Lamb down the middle of the great street of the city. On each side of the river stood the tree of life, bearing twelve crops of fruit, yielding its fruit every month. And the leaves of the tree are for the healing of nations.' **(Revelation 22:1-2)**

'Blessed are those who wash their robes, that they may have the right to the tree of life and may go through the gates into the city.' **(Revelation 22:14)**

APPENDIX 2

Key to Elements of Song of Songs with a New Covenant Perspective

(Song of Song Bible references are denoted by SS and references from The New Bible Dictionary (Douglas, 1962) as TNBD)

Apple: Heavenly fruit (see Apple tree) which delights, feeds and refreshes the Bride (*SS* 2:3&5) and later, when the Bride has matured, delights the Groom (*SS* 7:9); even the Bride's breath eventually emits the heavenly smell of apples (*SS* 7:8), because the heavenly is within her.

Apple tree: *(1) The Creator*. There is a sense of the Tree of Life at creation; in *SS* 2:3, the Groom (Jesus) is likened to an apple tree (see Groom); *(2) Mankind's origin*. According to which translation of *SS* you read, the apple tree is either the place where the Groom's mother conceived Him or it's the place where the Bride's mother conceived her (*SS* 8:5b). Personally, I read it as Jesus speaking to His Bride, reminding us of our heavenly beginnings of being conceived in Eden and of our original mother Eve. The Passion Translation (2020) agrees; *(3) True Vine*. For me, this is largely about Jesus as the Tree of Life (the True Vine), who offers us a fresh start, despite The Fall; *(4) Protection*. Like the feathers that cover us in Psalm 91:4, the Bride finds shade under the branches of the apple tree (*SS* 2:3); resting in God's protection.

Baal Hamon: The place of Solomon's vineyard (*SS* 8:11), which he rents out to tenants for a thousand shekels of silver. But the Bride doesn't rent from the King like a tenant. Rather, there is a sense in which the Bride herself is the fruit worth a thousand shekels, for she gives the Groom her vineyard (her heart) in its entirety (*SS* 8:12) and more for those who tend her fruit (i.e. those who help her to continue to produce good fruit).

Banner: The Bride recognises the Groom's banner over her as 'love' (*SS* 2:4). The Hebrew word for banner, in this instance, is the same one to describe the banners that marked each tribe of Israel (*TNBD*), bringing the focus on the Bride's acceptance into the Groom's family; just as we are spliced into the True Vine and made one with the God of love. The Groom describes the Bride as 'majestic as troops with banners' (*SS* 6:4), sitting well with the Bride of Christ in Revelation 19:6-8, rising up as one, beautiful, royal body. This resonates with Isaiah's description of Zion, i.e.

Jerusalem, as Bride to her Maker (Isaiah 49:18b and 54:5) and a banner to the nations (Isaiah 49:22). So, God is our banner and we are His.

Bath Rabbim: see Heshbon.

Beds: *(1) Spiritual torpor.* Beds are generally places of the Bride's soulishness and furniture from which she must arise, in exchange for the Groom's outdoor, heavenly realm; *(2) Earthly origins*: The Bride's mother's bed is the place where she was born, focussing on her earthly origin; *(3) Heavenly unity.* The only specified shared bed of the Bride and Groom is the one in *SS* 1:16-17, which is described in terms of trees, giving a sense of intimacy located in a private wood (in the great outdoors and therefore in heavenly territory; see Countryside and Fir).

Breasts: Deeply attractive to the Groom throughout, but also representative of the Bride's spiritual maturity and ability to sustain and grow others developing in the Faith (*SS* 8:10).

Bride: *(1) The Shulammite girl.* Brought into Solomon's harem (*SS* 6:13); *(2) Judah and Jerusalem*. God's chosen people (Isaiah 54:5); *(3) The Church.* The Bride of Christ (Ephesians 5:25).

Brothers: Representing the old guard, insisting the Bride neglect her own vineyard to look after the family vineyards of the Old Covenant; similar to the pharisaic response to Jesus. But the New Covenant isn't just about obeying laws; it's about coming into a loving relationship with the living God, which is characterised more by partnership than servitude. The finished work of the cross has dealt with sin; now it's all about giving our hearts to God, in order to bear much good fruit in Him; because everything good comes out of that.

Calamus: See Spices.

Carriage: Solomon's royal bridal carriage, made of precious woods and metals, inlaid with love (*SS* 3:9-10) and protected on every side (*SS* 3:7-8); very different to the subjugation of Pharaoh's Chariot of *SS* 1:9. There is a sense of rescue here and it's lavish; much like God sending Jesus to save us.

Carmel: See Mountains.

Cedar: An apt symbol of majesty and strength (*TNBD*) and a good companion to the fir trees mentioned in the couple's "house" in *SS* 1:17. Cedar was used to build Solomon's temple (*TNBD*), so the marital "house" of trees has a similar feel to Psalm 84:2, in which the writer longs to dwell in the house of the Lord, who is husband to His people (Isaiah 54:5). Also see Fir.

Chamber: the King's chamber is a place of intimacy and Psalm 27:4 echoes the desire of the psalmist, to seek the Lord in His dwelling place and gaze on His beauty.

Chariot: *(1) Entrapment.* In *SS* 1:9 the Bride is seen as a mare tethered to pharaoh's chariot, reflecting her early bound-up nature. *(2) The army of God.* Later on, the Groom is whisked away, by the Bride's maturing love, to the royal chariots of His people, which is suggestive of the Bride of Christ calling to her Groom and gathering to be part of the army of the Lord. Just as the Israelites escaped the chariots of Pharaoh's army to become a free people, so the Bride of Christ will rise up in maturity to declare freedom in Christ for all people; with their own land and their own chariots.

Chrysolite: See Topaz

Cinnamon: See Spices.

City: Manmade. A place to be rescued from and therefore likely to represent soulishness. The city is the place where those meant to protect you can end up hurting you (*SS* 5:7). The Groom is actually found in the city only once (*SS* 3:4), as a result of the sleepy Bride's excursion to find Him. Ever after, He is only found in gardens, orchards and countryside, though He enigmatically peers outside the Bride's bedroom window (*SS* 2:9) and knocks on the door (*SS* 5:2), ever calling His Bride to go with Him.

Cleft of the rock: In *SS* 2:14 the Bride is likened to a dove in the clefts of rock, where she is hiding. Fear holds back the Bride from knowing the Groom better. This is highly reminiscent of Moses being placed safely in the cleft of the rock to protect him from the deathly effects of seeing God's face (Exodus 33:20-23). But, in *SS* 2:14, the Groom implores the Bride to do the opposite and show Him her face and speak to Him. This points us all to the New Covenant relationship we have with Jesus, in which the indwelling Holy Spirit makes us safe in His presence. God promises, in Isaiah 43:2b, that we will not be burned by the flames of the fire; we have the fire of Holy Spirit within us and fire does not burn fire.

Countryside: Always heavenly in Song of Songs, representing the expanse of the Groom's Kingdom as territory to explore and nurture. The Groom's territory consists of hills (see Hills), mountains (see Mountains), woods (see Trees), orchards (see Fruit) and gardens (see Garden).

Damascus: A conquest of King David (2 Samuel 8:5-6), which must have still been under Solomon's dominion, at the time of writing *SS*. Damascus was rich in natural and commercial resources (*TNBD*), so when the Bride's nose is like the tower of Lebanon looking towards Damascus (*SS* 7:4) there is a sense of her coming into an expanded, rich and royal inheritance.

Daughters of Jerusalem: Faithful God-loving supporters.

Desert: Always indicative of the Israelites' forty years in desert; a time of preparation for the Promised Land. In spiritual terms, the desert represents soulishness (remember how the Israelites grumbled in Exodus 16:2-8). In *SS*, the desert is a place to be left behind, in exchange for spice-laden mountains (see Spices and Mountains).

Door: While the door of *SS* 8:9 represents, in a very small way, physical maturity for marital consummation (so the little sister must be protected until her wedding day), more significantly it relates to the kind of spiritual maturity that allows God access to one's heart. Furthermore, doors work both ways; we open our spiritual doors more and more to God, but also pass through more and more doors as we journey into Him.

Doves: *(1) Life and health*. In *SS* 1:15, the Groom describes the Bride's eyes as doves; presumably focussing on the bright and healthy whites of her eyes; *(2) Multiplication*. Cooing turtle doves in *SS* 2:12 allude to pairing, nesting and reproduction, in advance of the couple's marriage; *(3) Holy Spirit*. Represented as a dove in the Bible, highlighting the Bride's spirit-filled condition; *(4) Atonement*. Doves were used to atone for sin, emphasising the Bride's forgiven nature. The Groom sees the Bride as a perfect dove in *SS* 6:9.

Earrings: See Jewellery.

Eyes: In *SS* 1:15 and 4:1, the Groom tells the Bride that her eyes are doves (see Doves). The Bride's eyes are the first feature to capture the Groom's attention. In Matthew 6:22, Jesus says that the eye is the lamp of the body and that if they are healthy, our whole body will be full of life. Thus, the Groom is recognising spiritual life in His Bride's eyes. This spiritual maturity grows in such intensity by *SS* 6:5, that the Groom is overwhelmed by the Bride's eyes. By *SS* 7:4, the Bride has developed so much spiritually that her eyes have become like pools of water and therefore full of heavenly life (see Water). The Groom's eyes in 5:12 are likened to doves by 'the water stream', highlighting their life-giving nature (see Water). In *SS* 5:12, His eyes appeared as though washed in milk (see Milk); highlighting His purity.

Fawns: Twin fawns are used to describe the Bride's breasts, giving beautiful and tender symmetry; but also signifying the hope of future growth and expansion, through spiritually feeding others. (Also see Stag.)

Fig: See Fruit.

Fir: *(1) Evergreen.* Like the lovers of God in Psalm 1:3: *(2) Spiritual growth.* In Isaiah 41:19, firs are used to symbolise the desert becoming fertile (*TNBD*) and so make a good companion to the majesty and strength of cedar in the couple's "house" of *SS* 1:17; *(3) Place of intimacy.* The beams and rafters of the couple's "house" in *SS* 1:17, hanging over a verdant bed, suggest that the couple are lying on the grass looking up into the tops of the trees; a beautiful impression of intimacy, in heavenly countryside (see Countryside); *(4) Temple feature.* Both Fir (as Juniper, *TNBD*) and Cedar were used to build Solomon's temple of the Lord (2 Chronicles 3:5), highlighting that the Bride and Groom's union is a Godly one.

Fire: See Flame.

Flame: In *SS* 8:6 love is described like a blazing and mighty flame, which resonates with the many references to the fire of God in the Bible (Exodus 3:2, Exodus 13:21-22, Psalm 18:8, Ezekiel 1:4, Acts 2:3).

Fountain: See Water.

Foxes: Vermin that spoil the vineyards while they are in bloom and thus threaten the production of fruit. Spiritual vermin is anything that sets itself up against God (2 Corinthians 10:5), usually originating in soulishness. This is why we capture the little foxes, as we take every thought captive (see pages 20-22 on choosing how to think).

Fragrance: See perfume.

Fruit: Grapes and pomegranates are the main fruits of growth in the Bride's garden, although nuts, dates (fruit of the palm tree) and incense trees are also mentioned or alluded to. Development of fruit, in vineyards, orchards, nut groves and in palm trees, is all to do with stewarding the journey to spiritual maturity. The Groom (Jesus) regularly tests the ripeness of our fruit, to see how far along we are. It takes until *SS* 7:8 for the Bride's Breasts (see Breasts) to mature into bunches of fruit that are ready for harvesting.

Garden: There are three main forms of garden: *(1) The vineyard.* (*SS* 1:6 & 8:12). A form of garden, representing the Bride's heart, which she knows she needs to tend and then give to the Groom: *(2) The walled garden.* (*SS* 4:12-16). Represents the Bride's heart as maturing in readiness for release of the rich fragrances planted within her; *(3) Countryside.* Represents Heaven; the domain of God's garden (see Countryside), from where He is ever calling us to join Him. His garden is bigger, higher and safer than the

Bride's family vineyard (*SS* 1:6), where brothers intimidate, or than her soulish mountain tops (*SS* 4:8), where wild beasts stalk.

Gazelle: See Stag.

Gilead: See Goats.

Goats: Used to describe the Bride's flowing black hair, as cascading from Gilead; a place where Jacob and Laban made covenant together after their disagreements and also a place where balsam trees where grown for luxurious healing ointment (*TNBD*). This gives a strong sense of reconciliation and healing, flowing like long hair, as the Bride and Groom unite.

Goblet: The Bride's navel is described as a rounded goblet (*SS* 7:2), that never lacks blended wine and echoes Psalm 23:5, in which our cup overflows with God's blessings; how the Groom takes pleasure in the Bride's fullness. The navel is that abdominal hollow, which is a vestige of the newborn umbilical cord and therefore a constant reminder of our origin and heavenly design. How lovely that the Groom sees the Bride's navel as a goblet filled and overflowing with wine; how God loves His creation and its origin and how much more He has to give us!

Gold: signifies strength and preciousness, after refining and testing (proverbs 17:3). Gold signifies royalty and Heaven; the very street of Heaven is paved with gold (Revelation 21:21).

Groom: *(1) King Solomon. (SS 8:11); (2) God. (Isaiah 54:5); (3) Jesus. (Mark 2:19 & Ephesians 5:25).* The Passion Translation of *SS* describes the Groom as the 'Shepherd King', which echoes Jesus as Shepherd and Son of God.

Henna: See Perfume.

Heshbon: Clearly a place of beautiful pools, beside the gates of Bath Rabbim, to which the Groom likens the Bride's eyes (see Water and Eyes).

High Places: See Mountains.

Hills: Half-way heavenly places through which the Groom bounds from the mountains, to reach the Bride (*SS* 2:8); just as Jesus came down from on high, from Heaven to Earth.

Honeycomb: A fruit of the Promised Land (Exodus 3:8). The Bride's lips drop sweetness as the honeycomb (*SS* 4:11). Because God's Word is like honey (Psalm 119:103), it's as though the maturing Bride's own mouth is beginning to drip God's Word; heavenly and full of promise. Thus the Bride is coming into her spiritual inheritance.

House: *(1) The Bride's mother's house. (SS 3:4 and 8:2)* Signifies the Bride's earthly beginnings and surroundings. *(2) The al fresco house. SS* 1:16-17 represents the heavenly place, where the Bride and Groom find intimacy together (see Cedar and Fir).

Incense: Rather than signifying either Groom or Bride, incense denotes both Kingly gifts (SS 3:6) and Bridal growth (*SS* 4:14). God gives good gifts so that we, the Bride, produce good fruit (Galatians 5:22-23). Incense is used in anointing oil, burned with sacrifices in the Old Testament and is also associated with prayer, which rises like incense (Psalm 141:2), indicating that the Bride is approved, accepted and heard by the love of her life.

Ivory: The Bride describes the Groom's body as polished ivory (SS 5:14). Ivory was a mark of wealth (*TNBD*) and used to cover Solomon's throne (1 Kings 10:18), which emphasises the Groom's royal, white and blemish-free condition. In *SS* 7:4 the Groom depicts the mature Bride's neck as an ivory tower, ascribing beauty, worth and uprightness to her; she is developing royal and Godly qualities, which she did not possess in *SS* chapter 1.

Jerusalem: *(1) The place of God's presence.* Jerusalem is known as Zion, the place where the Lord is enthroned (Psalm 9:11) and dwells (Psalm 76:2). The ark of the covenant was brought to Jerusalem by David (1 Chronicles 13-15) and kept in the meeting place of the inner sanctuary, where God revealed His will to His servants and served as a symbol of God's presence (*TNBD*); *(2) God's presence in His Bride.* The Bride's description as being as lovely as Jerusalem (*SS* 6:4), speaks of God's presence in her heart; a prefiguring of the fulfilment of God's promise in Ezekiel 11:19 and 36:27 to put His Spirit in our hearts. Revelation 21:9-27 describes the Bride of Christ as the New Jerusalem, a beautiful and heavenly city. God dwells in His Bride and she in Him.

Jewellery: *(1) Elevation.* The Groom's gifts of jewellery (earrings and necklaces) to the bride elevate her from her lowly station, in the same way that we, as clay pots, are filled with God's treasure to showcase His all surpassing glory rather than our own (2 Corinthians 4:7). In Ezekiel 16:11-12 the Lord describes how He adorned His Bride, Israel, with jewels to augment her impoverished beginnings and make her beautiful before the nations; *(2) Lavish forgiveness.* Proverbs 25:12 says that the rebuke of a wise judge to a listening ear is like gold earrings (see also Silver). In *SS* 1:9, the Groom's gentle reproach is followed by His gift of earrings to His listening Bride. We have a prodigal God; recklessly extravagant towards us. Such bounty is a reminder of the spiritual riches of Heaven available to us, the very foundations of Heaven being jewels (Revelation 21:19-21); *(3)*

Victory. In *SS* 4:4 the Bride's necklace appears to have developed into a string of warrior shields, which indicates her growing maturity in spiritual combat and the rewards of battles hard won; *(4) Spiritual maturity*. The Groom sees the Bride's legs as crafted jewels (*SS* 7:1), readied for journeying with her husband into "the more" of God; *(5) God's glory*. The Bride describes the Groom's eyes as 'mounted like jewels' in *SS* 5:12, as she imagines Him face to face and is lost in wonder by the beauty of His heavenly eyes.

Lapis Lazuli: (Synonymous with Sapphire.) The Bride describes the Groom's body as decorated with lapis lazuli (*SS* 5:14). Lapis lazuli appears on the High Priest's breastpiece (Exodus 28:18). It is also one of the twelve heavenly foundations (Revelation 21:20) and this foundational meaning is echoed in Isaiah 54:13, all highlighting the priestly, heavenly and restorative nature of the Groom. Jesus is the great high priest (Hebrews 4:14-16) and the church's foundation stone (1 Corinthians 3:11).

Lebanon: An area with rich supply of cedars (*TNBD*). See Cedar and Mountains.

Lilies: *(1) Prized and beautiful*. The Groom describes the Bride as a lily among thorns in *SS* 2:2; she may be one of many, but He values her as the Lord values every hair on our heads (Matthew 10:30); *(2) The Bride's heart*. Lilies also epitomise *The Garden* of the Bride's heart, as a place where longing is fulfilled; as represented by grazing fawns among the lilies (*SS* 4:5). The Groom often walks among these lilies of the Bride's heart, gathering them up (*SS* 6:2), as a gardener might gather prized blooms for proud display of what has grown in His garden; *(3) The Word of God*. The Groom's lips are described as lilies by the Bride in *SS* 5:13. What characterises His mouth/words is also growing within her own lily-filled heart (see Mouth).

Mahanaim: Meaning the place of two camps (*TNBD*). In *SS* 6:13b, the Groom asks the friends why they would call back the Bride from being with the Groom and His people, as though she could possibly be in two camps at once, presumably implying that the Bride's journey towards unity with Groom must not be impeded or restricted. Radical obedience to God's will can be misunderstood by those who have our best interests at heart.

Mandrake: Known as the love apple (*TNBD*), which must have smelt heavenly, and which appears in *SS* 7:13 at the moment when the Bride has reached maturity and is ready to give everything she has to the Groom.

Marble: The Bride describes the Groom's legs as pillars of marble, reminiscent of the garden pillars at the king's palace in Esther 1:6, draped in material of royal purple (see Purple). This resonates with the purple upholstery of Solomon's wedding carriage and carries a lovely sense of strength and royalty, blended with beauty and love.

Milk: *(1) A fruit of the Promised Land*. (Exodus 3:8). Like honey, milk is under the Bride's tongue (*SS* 4:11). Milk was part of the staple diet of the Hebrews (*TNBD*) and its association in context with honey has similar meaning to Honeycomb (see Honeycomb); *(2) Health and light*. The Groom's eyes in *SS* 5:12 are as though they are 'washed in milk', the whiteness highlighting His health and youth, but also giving a sense of purity and inner light (see Eyes).

Moon: In *SS* 6:10 the Bride is described as fair as the moon, bright as the sun and as majestic as the stars in procession and corresponds to Psalm 8:3-8 in which, despite the wonder of the heavens' creation, God has crowned mankind with glory and honour. Also, the moon reflects the light of the sun, as we, the Bride, reflect the light of the Son.

Mouth: For kissing, eating, drinking and speaking. Spiritual passion, feeding, growing and intimacy abound, but it's not until the Bride matures that her own mouth develops the fragrance and sweetness of the Groom (see Apple and Honeycomb). Words are powerful in the Bible; when God spoke, the world came into being (Genesis 1:3). So the Bride's spiritual maturity brings new spiritual authority to the words of her mouth; when her uncertainty and torpor are left behind, she captures the vision and springs into action (*SS* 7:11-12).

Mountains: There are two kinds of high places, just as there are two trees in Eden: the high places, where other gods are worshipped (as denoted by Numbers 33:52 for example) and the spice-laden mountains (*SS* 8:14) of the One True God. The Bride begins her journey like a dove hiding on a mountainside, representing soulishness; the high places of the Old Testament being synonymous with idolatry. The Groom calls her down from the dangers of such high places in *SS* 4:8, where the beauty of Mounts Lebanon, Amana, Senir and Hermon conceal the dangers of lions and leopards (the devil walks around like a roaring lion in 1 Peter 5:8). The only way to get to the true and safe high places of God is to go with the Groom, who constantly calls us to join Him. In *SS* 7:5 the Bride's head is said to crown her like Mount Carmel, which means 'garden-land' (*TNBD*) and emphasises promise and her growing maturation in Godly wisdom and fruitfulness. When we capture every thought captive to the obedience of Christ, our minds become garden-lands, as well as our hearts. See the *Spirit to soul feedback loop*, on page 77.

Myrrh: See Perfume—Groom's.

Nard (Spikenard): See Perfume—Bride's.

Navel: See Goblet.

Neck: The Groom describes the Bride's neck as "the tower of David" (*SS* 4:4), which gives a sense of the Bride's redeemed spiritual uprightness and strength. This alludes to King David's Godliness and strength, which came from the Lord (Psalm 28:8).

Necklace: See Jewels.

North Wind: See Wind.

Nuts: See Fruit.

Orchard: See Fruit.

Palm: A tall and elegant tree, bearing clusters of dates. A symbol of stature and fruitfulness in *SS* 7:7, when describing the maturing Bride.

Perfume—Bride's: When the Bride's perfume spreads in the Groom's presence (*SS* 1:12-14), it seems to represent a mingling of their perfumes in advance of their wedding day and has a strong sense of spiritual awakening. Nard (Spikenard) is particularly representative of the Bride's perfume; this resonates strongly with Mary's breaking open of the pint of expensive nard over Jesus' feet, as a sign of her sacrificial and unfettered passion for her Lord in John 12:3. So, the Bride is at once highly treasured and also learning how to pour herself out for her Groom; this is the journey of the Church. There are many perfumes that grow in the enclosed garden of the Bride's heart in Chapter 4:12-15 of *SS*. In this walled garden, the fragrances intensify until the Bride is ready to release them for the benefit of others, whatever the season.

Perfume—Groom's: Jesus is described as the fragrance of God (Ephesians 5:1-2), so perfume poured out resonates with Christ pouring Himself out on the cross. Myrrh particularly signifies the Groom's perfume. The *TNBD* makes it clear that myrrh was not only used for embalming, but for holy anointing oil and for female purification rites and cosmetics; such a combination of meanings speaks of Jesus' holiness, His sacrificial passion on the cross and the cleansing and beautification it has brought to His Bride, the Church. The Groom's perfume is also beautiful like henna blossom, from the Vineyards of the oasis in En Gedi, reminding us that Jesus is the true vine and the water of life.

Pomegranate: Pomegranates have multitudinous seeds and, therefore, represent the promise of fruitfulness and multiplication. The Bride's temples are like pomegranates (*SS* 4:3). She wears a modesty veil over her face, making her temples a focus for attention. Pomegranates were much prized; crafted pomegranates were sewn onto the hem of the priestly garments (Exodus 28:33-34) and bronze pomegranates decorated the temple columns (2 Kings 25:17). To be compared to such a fruit gives a sense of the Bride being consecrated to the Groom.

Purple: Symbol of richness: purple cloth was costly to make and therefore a symbol of wealth and royalty (*TNBD*).

Raisins: Fruit of the vine (i.e. the True Vine) which strengthen the Bride (*SS* 2:5), as she lies enfolded in His arms (*SS* 2:6).

Raven: The Groom's hair is described by the Bride as black as a raven, emphasising His beauty and youth. While ravens don't always get a good press in the Bible, Noah sent a raven from the ark to test the waters (Genesis 8:7) and ravens were the birds that fed Elijah in the desert (1 Kings 17:4). I like the idea that even Jesus' hair represents the Good News and the Bread of Life.

Rose of Sharon: Used by the Bride to describe herself with humility, knowing she is beautiful and yet one of many; in fact the beauty of such flowers in the valley is in their sheer abundance, yet the Lord cherishes each and every one. While flowers are transient on earth, as Psalm 103:15-16 makes clear, when the Bride shelters under the apple tree (see Apple tree) in *SS* 2:3, she evokes not only her heavenly origin in Eden but, by default, her eternal heavenly inheritance.

Saffron: See Spices.

Sapphire: See Lapis Lazuli.

Sheep: Sheep are used to describe the whiteness of the Bride's teeth, i.e. her dazzling smile, as she looks at her Groom (*SS* 4:2 and 6:6). But these sheep are also just up from the washing, which gives a sense of the Bride being freshly washed by the blood of the Lamb.

Shepherd: Seekers of Christ, the Good Shepherd; those also in search of God (*SS* 1:8).

Shulammite: Solomon's counterpart (*TNBD*).

Silver: Proverbs 25:4 says 'Remove the dross from the silver, and a silversmith can produce a vessel', so silver is highly symbolic of atonement through a process of refinement.

South Wind: See Wind.

Spices: Expensive, used for food preparation, flavouring of wines and embalming (*TNBD*). Proverbs (written by Solomon, the author of *SS*) 7:17 makes it clear that myrrh, aloes and cinnamon were used to perfume marital beds. Spices appear in the marriage procession of *SS* 3:6 and also in the Bride's walled garden of *SS* 4:14 and symbolise the couple's mutual wedding gifts of great worth and honour, until death do they part. Myrrh, cinnamon and calamus were also used in anointing oil (Exodus 30:23-25) and give a sense of matrimonial consecration. The spice-laden mountains of *SS* 8:14 combine a sense of rich growth and the high places of God, to describe the place the Bride has come to on her consecrated journey into God.

Spikenard (Nard): See Perfume—Bride.

Spring: *(1) Season*. A time for new spiritual growth, *(2) Water.* (See Water).

Stag: *(1) Climber of mountains*. The Stag on the hills (SS 2:8-9) represents the Groom and therefore Jesus; swift and graceful, as in Psalm 18:33. He calls His Bride up higher (but down from any idolatry) and grazes in *The Garden* of the Bride's heart. *(2) Bridegroom*. The Groom as stag (or gazelle *SS* 2:9) makes the Bride His doe (or gazelle *SS* 4:5). There is a strong correlation here between Proverbs 5:19, in which the doe is a wife whose breasts satisfy and intoxicate her love, and *SS* 8:10 in which the Bride's breasts bring contentment to the King. Because the Bride is the stag's doe, as in Psalm 42:1, she thirsts for Him. As she learns to run with Him, 'He makes [her] feet like the feet of a deer; He causes [her] to stand on the heights' (Psalm 18:33)—see Mountains. *(3) Purity*. Deer are considered clean animals (Deuteronomy 12:22); the Groom is pure.

Stars: See Moon.

Sun: See Moon.

Tirzah: *(1) Beautiful town*. The Groom describes the Bride as beautiful as Tirzah, which was a delightful town captured from the Canaanites by Joshua (Joshua 12:24). *(2) Inheritance*. Tirzah was also Zelophehad's youngest of five daughters, who, in Numbers 27:1-7 successfully claimed their father's inheritance after he died without male issue (*TNBD*). This echoes the Bride of Christ's inheritance of the Kingdom, as given by a good and loving Father God.

Topaz: (Synonymous with Chrysolite.) The Bride describes the Groom's arms as set with topaz (*SS* 5:14), which is one of the twelve stones on the High Priest's breastpiece (Exodus 28:20) and one of the foundations of

Heaven (Revelation 21:20), thereby emphasising how precious and heavenly they are. Topaz also appears on the heavenly intersecting wheels in Ezekiel 1:16 and 10:9, the rims full of eyes, echoing the Groom's all-seeing nature.

Tower: Strengthened city walls, which offered vantage points of defence (*TNBD*), adding prophetic meaning to the Bride's mature position as warrior and "watchman".

Trees: see Apple tree, Beds, Cedar, Fir, Fruit, Incense, Palm and Garden.

Vineyard: representation of Israel, but also of the heart. A place which needs regular tending to protect it from neglect or damage from interfering influences (*SS* 1:6, 2:15).

Wall: *(1) God filled.* Like the walls of Jerusalem. God calls Jerusalem His throne in Jeremiah 3:17. The New Jerusalem is described 'as a bride adorned for her husband' (Revelation 21:2) and the walls are made of jasper (Revelation 21:18), which resonates with John's description of the one sitting on the throne like jasper (Revelation 4:3). *(2) Spiritual strength.* The Passion Translation (2020) of *SS* 8:10 makes sense of this: 'But now I have grown and become a bride, and my love for Him has made me a tower of passion and contentment for my beloved. I am now a firm wall of protection for others, guarding them from harm. This is how he sees me - I am the one who brings Him bliss, finding favour in His eyes'. Isaiah 54:11-12 echoes a similar process of the Bride being rebuilt with righteousness.

Watchmen: There are two types of watchmen: the earthly city guards who are supposed to protect the inhabitants of the city and spiritual elders who are supposed to guide the faithful. The old guard, holding onto the Old Covenant, as opposed to the New, have a tendency to hurt seekers of God (*SS* 5:7). Nevertheless, in *SS* 8:10, the mature Bride becomes like a watch tower of spiritual strength and wisdom, for the benefit of all on their quest for God.

Water: Always represents life. The Bride is described as a 'spring enclosed, a sealed fountain' (*SS* 4:12), alluding to spiritual blockage. Later, she is seen as 'a garden fountain, a well of flowing water [from the river of life], streaming down from Lebanon' (*SS* 4:15). The change from blocked to flowing resonates strongly with Jesus' assertion that anyone who drinks from Him will become 'a spring of water welling up to eternal life' (John 4:13). The Groom's eyes are like water streams (*SS* 5:12), full of eternal life. *SS* 8:7 makes it clear that many earthly waters cannot quench God's vast sea of life.

Well: See Water.

Wheat: The Bride's waist is described as a mound of wheat (*SS* 7:2). Wheat represents God's bounty and was also used as a sacrificial offering (*TNBD*), giving a sense of lavish libation.

Wind: In *SS* 4:16, the north wind or south wind (*SS* 4:16) indicate difficulties or blessings respectively, the north wind being typically bitterly cold and the south wind warm.

Wine: *(1) Sacrifice.* The lovers' passion for one another is considered greater than wine in *SS* 1:2 and 4:10 and gives a sense of abstinence in exchange for the greater thing. The blood of Christ is symbolised by the communion wine, representing sacrificial love. *(2) The coming of the Kingdom of God.* Jesus says He would not drink of the fruit of the vine until He drinks it with us in His Father's Kingdom (Matthew 26:29); the shedding of Jesus' blood and the sending of Holy Spirit suggests that the greater thing has come and is now; Heaven is within the Bride and that means us.

Wilderness: See Desert.

Winter: The time when there is no growth. In *SS* 2:11, Jesus calls us out of this inert state, into spiritual growth and fruitfulness. The time is now.

APPENDIX 3
Fifteen Promises of God

Here are fifteen scriptural promises (in no particular order), to help you focus on what God has planted in your heart. However, there are thousands of promises in the Bible and 'no matter how many promises God has made, they are 'Yes' in Christ' (2 Corinthians 1:20). God has so much for you and it's all good.

I would encourage you to read the Bible daily and take note of any scriptures that particularly "speak" to you. When you have collected a few verses, order them appropriately and string them together in the form of a prayer. Then declare your prayer aloud daily. It is remarkable how such a crafted prayer can change your circumstances, as well as your outlook.

1. **God's promises never fail**: 'Not one of all the Lord's good promises to Israel failed; every one was fulfilled.' (Joshua 21:45)

2. **God is always good**: 'You are good and what You do is good; teach me Your decrees.' (Psalm 119:68)

3. **God is always with me:** 'Have I not commanded you? Be strong and courageous. Do not be afraid; do not be discouraged, for the Lord your God will be with you wherever you go.' (Joshua 1:9)

4. **God is faithful:** 'Let us hold unswervingly to the hope we profess, for He who promised is faithful. (Hebrews 10:23)

5. **God is kind and compassionate**: '"Though the mountains be shaken and the hills be removed, yet My unfailing love for you will not be shaken nor My covenant of peace be removed", says the Lord, who has compassion on you.' (Isaiah 54:10)

6. **God designed me for a purpose:** 'For we are God's handiwork, created in Christ Jesus to do good works, which God prepared in advance for us to do.' (Ephesians 2:10)

7. **God loves me deeply, no matter what**: 'For I am convinced that neither death nor life, neither angels nor demons, neither the present nor the future, nor any powers, neither height nor depth, nor anything else in all creation, will be able to separate us from the love of God that is in Christ Jesus our Lord.' (Romans 8:38-39)

8. **God gives me power for my life**: 'For the Spirit God gave us does not make us timid, but gives us power, love and self-discipline.' (2 Timothy 1:7)

9. **God's presence brings joy:** 'You make known to me the path of life; You will fill me with joy in Your presence, with eternal pleasures at Your right hand.' (Psalm 16:11)

10. **God will fill me to overflowing with hope:** 'May the God of hope fill you with all joy and peace as you trust in him, so that you may overflow with hope by the power of the Holy Spirit.' (Romans 15:13)

11. **God will strengthen and help me:** 'So do not fear, for I am with you; do not be dismayed, for I am Your God. I will strengthen you and help you; I will uphold you with my righteous right hand." (Isaiah 41:10)

12. **God will give you wisdom**: 'If any of you lacks wisdom, you should ask God, Who gives generously to all without finding fault, and it will be given to you.' (James 1:5)

13. **God promises you an abundant life**: 'The thief comes only to steal and kill and destroy; I have come that they may have life, and have it to the full.' (John 10:10)

14. **God has a plan for my life**: '"For I know the plans I have for you," declares the Lord, "plans to prosper you and not to harm you, plans to give you hope and a future."' (Jeremiah 29:11)

15. **God fights my battles:** 'You shall not be afraid of them; the Lord your God himself will fight for you.' (Deuteronomy 3:22)

Bibliography:

Arnott, J. & C. (2012) *Grace and Forgiveness*, New Wine Press: Weybridge

Bixler, O. (2016) *It Isn't Free And It Isn't Masonry*, Sovereign World Ltd: Ellel, Lancaster; first published by Zaccmeida

Cooke, G. (2007) *Prophecy and Responsibility*, Brilliant Book House; Vacaville

Cooke, G. (2015) *Jesus Demanded Graham Cooke, "Give Me back My stuff!"*; YouTube: https://youtu.be/A-dBioGxk0E

Cooke, G. (2016) *God Doesn't See What Is Wrong With You*, Articles: Brilliant Perspectives

Cooke, G. (2022) *Relational Learning*, Podcast: Brilliant Perspectives

Cooke, G. (2023) *Grace is God's empowering presence*, Brillianttv.com

Davidson, M. (2010) *Becoming the Beloved; the End Time Bride of Christ*, Shulamite Ministries Publishing. USA

Douglas, J. (1962) *The New Bible Dictionary*, Intervarsity Fellowship: London

Gossett, D. (1976) *What You Say is What You Get!* Bold Bible Missions: Blaine, WA

Huggett, J. (1996) *Listening to Others*, Hodder & Stoughton Ltd: London

Johnson, Beni (2013) *The Happy Intercessor*, Destiny Image Publishing Inc: Shippensburg PA

Johnson, Bill. (2018) *Stewards of the Divine*, YouTube: https://youtu.be/fGXKdPBV9LU

Johnson, Bill. (2022) *Breaking the Bread of my Soul*, YouTube: https://youtu.be/LbmKDFcG-vE

Johnson, Bill. & Valloton, K. (2006) *The Supernatural Ways of Royalty*, Destiny Image Publishers, Inc: Shippensburg PA

Lewis, C. (2009) *The Last Battle*, Harper Collins Children's Books: London, New York; first published by The Bodley Head 1956

Nee, W. (1995) *The Song of Songs*, Living Stream Ministry: Anaheim, Ca

New International Version, *The Bible*; British Text eBook Edition of the Bible, Hodder & Stoughton

Otis, G. (1997) *The Twilight Labyrinth: Why does Spiritual Darkness Linger Where it does?* Chosen Books: Grand Rapids

Pierce, C. (2014) *Healing Rooms Ministries Team Training*, official training video

Pierce, C. (2015) *Destroying Cancer*, YouTube: https://youtu.be/9saqUUNXock

Prince, D, (2013) *Pulling Down Strongholds*, Derek Prince Ministries-UK: Baldock

Rohr, R. (2003) *Everything Belongs*, The Crossroad Publishing Company: New York

The Passion Translation (New Testament with Psalms, Proverbs, and Song of Songs (2020), Broad Street Publishing Group, LLC
Sobel, J. (2022) *The Chosen, Round Table (S1, E2),* The Chosen App
Sobel, J. (2023) *The Chosen, Round Table (S2, E2),* The Chosen App
Virkler, M. (2013) *Four Keys to Hearing God's Voice,* Destiny Image Publishers, Inc: Shippensburg
Wren James, C. (2012) *Beyond Prophetic,* Life Streams International: Australia
Wren James, C (2014) *Naked I Stand,* Life Streams International: Australia
Young, W. (2008) *The Shack*, Hodder Windblown: UK; first publish US 2007
Zoe (2023) *Personalised Nutrition*, Health App in association with Kings College London

Recommended Reading:

Bevere, J. (2014) *The Bait of Satan*, Charisma House: Lake Mary
The importance of not taking offence

Carothers, M. (2010) *Prison to Praise,* Hodder & Stoughton; first published in UK 1970
The power of giving thanks in and for all circumstances

Joyner, R. (2017) *There were Two Trees in the Garden*, Morning Star Publications: Fort Mill
Understanding the battle raging for the heart and soul of every human being

Thompson, A. & Beale, A (2011) *The Divinity Code to understand your dreams and visions*, Destiny Image Publishers, Inc: Shippensburg
A handy dictionary for interpreting dreams and visions

INDEX:

Abstract, thinking, 25, **27**
Acupuncture, potential block, 101
Adam, 6, 7, 20, 21, 35, 50
Al fresco, spiritual territory, 38, 52
Alive, to God, **74-75**
American football, analogy, 113
Angel wing, imagined, 24
Anorexia, 102
Apostolic, mature Bride, 57
Arch, 45, 46
Armour of God, 44, 77, **113**
Astral projection, ungodly, 11
Authority, in Christ, 57, 61, 86, 105, 116

Baggage, we all have it, 13, 46, 60
Balancing pole, tightrope walking, 31
Baptism, dying to self, 9
Battle, spiritual, of the mind, 23, 46, 99, 100, 112-113, 117, 131 (Jewellery), 140 (Deuteronomy), 142 (Joyner)
Beach, 45, 117
Bear, imagining God as, 66
Bed, four poster, 46
Bed, spiritual torpor, 53, 55-56, **126 (Beds)**
beelzebub, 12, see endpaper footnote
Bethel Sozo, 117
Bixler, Otto, 111
Blessing, as in spiritual warfare, **114**
Blocks, to entering *The Garden*: also see Resistance

Boat, 46
Body, soul & spirit, **6-7**, 69
Boot, out the bad, 22, 105, 116

Brain, hardware in need of surrendering, 6, 77
Brain changing, 29, 77
Bride, **49-60**
Bridge, crossing to new self, 13-14
Bridging gaps, in intercession, 101
Buddhism, more a philosophy, 11-12

Careless talk, 21
Carriage, 45-46, 54, 56, **126 (Carriage)**, 133 (Marble)
Casual spiritual approach, 67
Childlike trust, **13**, 13, 18, 40, 44
Choice, originally heavenly, 20
Choice, ungodly, 7, **20-22**
Chosen, in Christ, 55, 57, 73, 97, 114, 115
Citizen, of Heaven, 6, 37, **39**
City, old self/ways, 54, 56, 127 (City), 137 (Watchmen)
Clay pots, 3
Closed door, to *The Garden*, 96, 98
Co-labour, with God, 22, 32, 50, 67, 77, 91
Communion, 5, 116, 138 (Wine)
Compassion, in intercession, 101-102
Complaining, grumbling, 21
Composite, with God (New creation), 17
Compost heap, 43-44, 45
Concrete thinking, 25, **26**
Condemnation, none in Christ, 32, 75, 81
Confidentiality, 88, 102
Contamination, in *The Garden*, 13, 99
Contemplation, 11, 12
Control, self-imposed, 12

Cooke, Graham, 10-11, 15, 18, 75, 97
Counterfeits, identifying, 11-12
Countryside, heavenly territory, 52, 54, 57, 126 (Beds), 127 (City, Countryside), 129, (Garden)
Crafted, prayer, 139
Creative imagination, 18, 25, 28
Creative thinking, 18, 25, 28, **30**
Creativity, not to be quashed, **19-20**
Criticism, 21, 97
Cross, key to the heart, 5
Cross, the answer to life, 21, 44
Curiosity, spiritual, 67
Curriculum, spiral, **73-78**
Curses, causes and antidotes, 100, **112-114**

Dabbling, in the occult, 100, also see Slime & Ungodly
Dahlia, daughter symbol, 67
Darkness, imagined in *The Garden*, 81, 96-97, 98
Darkness, ungodly elements in *The Garden*, 12
Davidson, Mark, 49
Death, origin/fear of, 20-21, 61
Deep, calls to deep, 50
Desert, dying to self, 54, 128 (Desert)
Development, spiritual, see Growth
Difficulties, journeying through, 62, **63**
Dimensions, perspective, 37, 75
Dirty rags, 75
Discouraging words, 21
Disunity, in the body of Christ, 56
Divine exchange, replacing dark with God's light/Word/promises, 22, 57, 68, 105, 118,
Divine, pursuit (journeying with God), 10

Door, to our heart, 5
Door, closed to *The Garden*, 96, 98
Dream, Graham Cooke's, 97
Dream interpretation, 142 (Thompson & Beale)
Dreaming, abstract/creative ability, 20, 25, 28, 29
Dreaming, good things, 19
Dreams, Gods, 18, 20
Druid, as red herring, 12
Dying to self, 9, 18, 64, 74-75

Eating, see Feasting
Eden, *The Garden* of, 6, 7,12, 35, **36**, 37, 57, 73, 84, 125 (Apple tree), 133 (Mountains), 135 (Rose of Sharon)
Egg, story of, 33
Ego, the old self, 12
Emmanuel, God with us, 21
Encounter, with God, see Intimacy
End-point will, 47
Enemy assignments, prayer against, **114**
Enlargement, of the heart, **49-58, 73-78**, 80
Esteem, low, 32, 87, **97-98**
Eternity, 3, 10, 12, 14, 75
Eve, 6, 7, 20, 21, 35, 50
Exploration, Heavenly pursuit, 47, 52, 90
Explorer, with facilitator in ministry, 87-104
Eyeball, analogy for dark and light, 74-75
Ezekiel, *lectio divina*, 76

Face God, spiritual warfare, 60, 99, **113**
Facilitator; leading explorers in *The Garden* as ministry, **87-104**
Faith, Christ dwells in us through, 3, 8

Faith, having/growing in, 3, 8, 55, 75-77
Faith, imagination (creative and opening heavenly doors), 2, 10, 20, 21, 25, 28-29, 37, 64-65, 77-78
Faith, imagination (how to grow in it), 25
Faith, journey, 18
Faith, new in the, 96
Faith, sapped by facing the enemy, 99-100
Faith, shield of, 113
Faith, saved by professing our, 105
Faithful, God is, 139 (Hebrews)
Fall, the, 6, 7, 20, 73, 125 (Apple Tree)
Father, God, 3, 4, 5, **8**, 9, 10, 22, 40, 46
Fear, causes and antidotes, 10, 13, 19-20, 21-22, 46, 61-62, 87, 99, **108-110, 112-114**, 127 (Cleft of the rock), 139-140 (Joshua, Romans, 2 Timothy, Isaiah, Deuteronomy)
Fear, shock and trauma, 99, **108-110**
Feasting, revelation, intimacy, sustenance, picnic, 52, 55, 66, 71-72, 86
Feedback loop, spirit to soul, **77-78**
Foray, spiritual pursuit, 2, 10-11, 29, 35, 37, 52, 94
Forest, 80, 86
Forget-me-nots, 81
Forgiveness, 100, **110-111**
Formal garden, 45
Fountain, 45, 81
Foxes, spoiling the vineyard, 53, 129 (Foxes)
Freedom in Christ course, 98, **117**
Freedom, in God, 13, 20, 55

Freemasonry, 100, also see Slime & Ungodly
Fullness, in God, 15, 71, 130 (Goblet)

Galilee, Sea of, 47
Gaps, in knowledge and how to fill them, 20
Garden, re Heaven, **4**
Garden, (The) what it isn't, **11-12**
Garden, ungodly, 11-12
Gardener, The (Father God), 10, 123 (John)
Geyser, the horse, 44-45
Giverny, Monet's water garden, 94-95
Gnomes, ungodly, 12
Gossett, Don, 25, 97
Gossip, 21
Grafted, into the true vine, 8, 22
Grief, **61-62, 96-97**, 105-107
Groom, God as, **49-60**, also see Husband
Grove, inner, ungodly, 12
Growth, spiritual, 8, 47, **49-60, 73-78**, 87, 128 (Fawns), 129 (Fruit), 131 (Incense), 136 (Spices and Spring)
Grumbling, 21,

Harry Potter, ungodly influence, 100, 111, also see Slime & Ungodly
Healing, 23-24, 32, **105-118**
Healing on the Streets, 54
Healing Rooms, 117
Health, see Wellbeing
Hearing God, **32**, 94
Heaven, down to Earth, 7, 102
Heaven, where is it? **3**, 73-75
Hedge, 44-45
High places, Godly/ungodly, 54, **133 (Mountains), 136 (Spices)**

Holiness, God's, 22, 134 (Perfume, Groom's)
Holy Spirit, in us, 6-9, 73
Homeland, ours (Heaven), 6, also see Citizen
Hope, 22, 44, 62, 92, 98, 115, 140 (Jeremiah)
Hopelessness, by facing the enemy, 99
Horoscopes, ungodly, 100, also see Slime & Ungodly
Horse, the white, 44-45
Huggett, Joyce, 19, 24
Humanism, independent of God, 6
Husband, God as, **49-60**, 73, 126 (Cedar), 131 (Jewellery), 136 (Wall)

'I know', Painting of Jesus, 104
Identity, true, 2, 6-9, **14**, 74-75, 98, 115
Illness, as a block, 98
Image, God's (made in and being transformed into), 16, 20, 21, 74-75
Imagination, cast down vain, 19
Imagination, heavenly weapon, **23**
Imagination, inner healing, **23-24**
Imagination, no threat to Biblical redaction, 19-20
Imagination, problematic, **31-34**
Imagination, safe spiritual tool, **17-24**
Immersive, experience of *The Garden*, 2, 37, 50-51, 61-63, 90
Inexperience, ungodly, **109**
Inheritance, heavenly, 2, 3, 6, 37, 74, 136 (Tirzah)
Inheritance, of all God's estate, 6
Inkling, God's thinking in the, 41, 101
Inner grove, as red herring, 12
Inner healing, 23-24, **105-118**
Intel, heavenly, 101

Interfacing, with God, 22
Intellect, 6, also see Thinking
Interactive space, *The Garden*, 2, **10**, 17
Intercession, utilising *The Garden*, **101-103**
Intercourse, spiritual vs carnal, 50
Intimacy, encounter with the Lord/Word, 19, 37, 43-47, 49-**60**, 94, 99, 127 (Chamber)
Israel/Israelites, 21, 40, 49, 52, 54, 119 (Numbers), 121 (Isaiah), 122 (Hosea, Amos), 125 (Banner), 127 (Chariot), 128 (Desert), 131 (Jewellery), 137 (Vineyard), 139 (Joshua)

Jars, (pots) of clay, 3, 131 (Jewellery)
Jesus, *'I know'*, by Sarah McCrum, 104
Jesuits, 20
Jesus Ministry conference, 66
Johnson, Beni, 113
Johnson, Bill, 3, 11, 18, 33, 110, 112
Journey will, 47
Journeying, spiritual travel/divine pursuit, 92, **49-60**

Kedar, tents of, 46
Keeping your healing, 115
Kick starting, imagination, **33-34**
Kingdom, in our hearts, 3, 4, 6-9
Kitten, imagining self as, 66

Lapis lazuli, (sapphire) pavement, 45-46
Learning, relational, **10-11**, 21, also see Curriculum
Learning, Scripture by heart, **64**
Learning, spiritual, 2, 3, 14, 29, 37, 87

Learning, student centred, **19**, also see Curriculum
Learning, to walk in Scripture, **64**
Leave to cleave, spiritual journeying, 53
Leave to seek, the spiritual journey, 52
Lectio divina, 28, **35, 39, 63, 76**
Legal spirituality, 86
Lewis, C.S., 37, 76
Life, God as author and giver of, 7
Lighthouse, 59
Lilies, 95, **132 (Lilies)**
Lily, symbol of daughter, 67
Litmus test, imaginative ability, 29, **30**
Logic, 18
Love, also see Perfect love
Low self esteem, 32, 87, **97**

Mansion, 45
Marx, Mark, 54
Meditation, 11, 12-13
Memes, spiritual, 101
Midrash, re imagination, 20
Mind, part of the soul, 6-7
Mind, renewal, **17-22**
Mind, spirit of, 22
Mind of Christ, 2, 10, 21, 28, 32
Ministry, *The Garden* as a tool, **87-104**
Moaning, 24, 146 (Desert)
Monet, Claude (Lily pond at Giverny), 95
Mortal experience, 22
Mountain, 1, 40, 41, 46, 53, 66, 84, 133 (Mountains)

Natural instinct, as opposed to Godly, 74-75
Nee, Watchman, 49
Negativity, 21, 22, 60, 67, 97, 116
Neuroplastic, brain changing, 29, 77

New Age, ungodly, 11
New beginnings, journeying, 67, 79
New creation, 3, 7, 8, **9**, 13, 17, **74-75**
Non Christians, re *The Garden*, 103
Nose, Jesus', 68
Nun, frightened film character, 61

Obstruction, imaginative and spiritual, **31, 96-111**
Occult, dangers and antidotes, 16, 100-101, **111-115**, 117-118
Old, self/instinct, 12-13, 74-75
Orchard, of the heart, 59, 82
Original design, in God, 6-9, 74
Otis, George, 101
Ouija board, ungodly, 100, also see Slime
Outdoors, heavenly territory, 38, 126 (Beds), 127 Countryside)

Palace, 45
Palm reading, ungodly, 100, also see Slime & Ungodly
Perfect love, antidote to fear, 13, 24, 53
Perfume, **134 (Perfume)**
Permissible pleasures, 86
Perseverance, **32-33**, 97-98, 110
Pessimism, 21, also see Negativity
Pharisaic thinking, 52, 56, 126(Brothers)
Picnic, 1, 66, 71
Pictures, visualisation, 2, 17, 20, 27, **29, 34**, 43, 77
Pierce, Cal, 60, 99, 113
Pixies, ungodly, 12
Play, essential for growth, 11, 45, 66, 80, 87
Plays, American football term, 113
Positives, God's, 22, 60, 67, 97-98, 116
Prayer Line, National, 117

Prince, Derek, 9
Process, *The Garden* is a, 47
Promised Land, 54, 55, 128
  (Desert), 130 (Honeycomb), 133
  (Milk)
Promises, of God-in spiritual
  warfare, 78, 100, 115, 139
  (Joshua, Isaiah, Romans), 140
  (Isaiah & Deuteronomy),
Psalm 23, **61-72, 65, 87-92**
PTSD, 94-95

Rainbow, 40, 41, 44, 77
Reason, intellect, 18
Relational learning, **10-11**, 19,
  also see Curriculum
Relationship, with God, 18, 19, 20,
  29, **49-60**
Religions, other, 101
Remembering, spiritual tool, **38-33, 56**
Renewal, spiritual, 2, also see
  entire manual
Repent, meaning, 21
Resistance to *The Garden*, **95-101**
Restoring the Foundations, 118,
Revelation 4, being there, **37-41**
Robes, heavenly, 75, 77, 92
Rohr, Richard, 15

Sanctified, imagination, see Faith
  imagination
Sand castles, 45
Sapped, faith/hope (by facing the
  enemy, 99-100
Sapphire, (lapis lazuli) pavement,
  5-46
Satan[ii], 12, 13, 21, 22, 46, 99, 112,
  also see endpaper footnote
Scotland, creative picture of, 28
Scripture, learning by heart, **64**
Scripture, walking in it, **36, 39, 51, 63**
Sea, of crystal/glass, 40, 46, 77

Sea, of Galilee, 46-47
Searching, see Silver
Seed, as the Word, 4
Seedlings, 82
Seeker's prayer, 16
Self, old, 12-13, 74-75
Self worth, 19
Self esteem, low, 32, 87, **97-98**
Servitude, as old way of thinking,
  52, 126 (Brothers)
Shack, The, 66
Shed, 45
Shoots, green, 82
Silver, searching for God, 10, 35
Sin, 16, **98-99**
Sleepiness, spiritual torpor, 53
Slime, spiritual, **98-101**, 112
Sobel, Jason, 20, 73
Soil, re the heart, **4**, 103
Song of Songs, **49-60, 125-138**
Soul, body & spirit, **6-9**, 69
Soul ties, 70, **105-108**
Soulishness, 14, 22, 52, 53, 75, 126
  (Beds), 127 (City), 128 (Desert),
  129 (Foxes, Garden), 133
  (Mountains)
Sozo, 117
Speaking, the Word aloud, 61, 105
Spiral curriculum, spiritual
  learning/journey, **75-77**
Spirit, body & soul, **6-9**, 69
Spirit, of the mind, 22
Spiritual torpor, 53
Spirituality, legal 86
Spouse's garden, **59**
Stacking dolls, the Trinity, **8**
Storm, 47
Strength, from God, 134 (Raisins),
  137 (Wall), 140 (Isaiah)
Stuff, "give me back my", 97
Submarine, 102
Sundial, 82

Surrender, to God, 2, 9, 10, 11, 12, 20, 21, 22, 23, 29, 54, 57, 75, 77, 78, 84, 94, 98, 101, 102, 105
Swearing, bad habit, 46, 99
Sword, in Jesus' mouth, 43

Talmud, Jewish, 86
Tardis, 10
Tents, of Kedar, 46
Tents, tabernacle/body, **73-74**
Territory, (spiritual/heavenly estate or homeland), re the spiritual heart, 2, 6, **10**, 49, **64-65**
Testing, spiritual challenge, 20, 47, 55, **73-77**, 129 (Fruit), 130 (Gold)
Thanksgiving, in spiritual warfare, 116
Thinking, after heart response to God, **10**
Thinking, choosing how to, **20-22**, 31
Thinking, earthly vs heavenly— Kingdom thinking, 6, 10, 31, 49, 70-71, 116, also see Brain
Thinking, previously learned /former patterns of, 13, 21, 57
Thinking, God's (identifying), 32, 41, 101
Thinking, negatively, 21, 22, 97, 99, 116, 129 (Foxes), also see Divine exchange
Tightrope, heavenly journey, **31**, 71
Torpor, spiritual, 53
Transformation, spiritual, 5, 14, 17, 18-19, 117
Treasure (silver included), us/in us, the search for, 4, 10, 11, 13, 23, 35, 52, 55, 74, 86, 125, 131 (Jewellery)
Trees, the two, 35, also see Eden
Trinity, God, **8**
Trinity, self, **6-9**

True self, identity, 2, 6-9, **14**, 74-75, 98, 115
True vine, 8, 22, 125 (Apple tree, Banner), 134 (Perfume), 135 (Raisins)
Trust, confidence in *The Garden*, 38
Trust, in God or self, 11, 12-13, 18, 20-22
Truth, God's perspective (the Cross, the Word), 18, 19, 43, 61
Tulips, 83

Unforgiveness, as a block, **100, 100-111**
Ungodly, elements/behaviours, 12, 20, 60, 100-101
Unity, the body of Christ, 56
Unity, with/in God, **7-9**

Vagueness, in hearing God, 32, 41, 101
Valloton, Kris, 110
Vicious circles, **78**
Vine, see True vine
Vineyard, the spiritual heart (ours and God's), 52, 53, 58, 125 (Baal Hamon), 126 (Brothers), 129 (Foxes, Fruit, Garden), 134 (Perfume), 137 (Vineyard)
Virkler, Mark, 22, 32
Visualisation, spiritual tool, **18-19, 29**

Waking, to God, 17, 25, 56, 74-75, 134 (Perfume)
Walking in Scripture, 2, **36, 39, 51, 63**
Walled garden, re spiritual heart, 55, **79-83, 92-93, 129 (Garden)**
War trauma, **94-95**
Warfare, spiritual, see Battle, Face God, Promises, Thanksgiving

Watchmen, 54, 56, 137 (Watchmen)
Waterfall, 1, 44, 84
Watson, David, 19
Waves, 47
Wellbeing, 9, 115
Will, journey/end point, 47
Windsock, 81
Witchcraft, occult, 16, 100, **111-115**, 117-118
Wood, forest/trees, 35, 45, 52, 66, 68, 80, 125 (Apple tree), 126 (Beds, Cedar), 128 (Fir), 129 (Fruit), 134 (Palm)
Word, (spoken) in spiritual warfare, 61,105,115
Worth, self, 19
Wren, Chris James, 1, 47, 78

Yes, to God's and God's, 15, 21, 22
Yoga, ungodly, 101
Young, William, 66

Zen Buddhism, more a philosophy, 11-12
Zoe, app, 77

About the Author:

Rev Ruth Scorey is ordained as a minister with Healing Rooms Ministries; a worldwide Christian organisation, headed up by Cal Pierce in Spokane, USA, for anyone seeking healing in mind, body and spirit. Ruth was born in Birmingham, UK, the fifth of six children, to Roman Catholic parents. She first heard God speak at the age of eight; not an audible voice or a voice in her head, but rather as a very strong internal impression of someone good and utterly trustworthy. The voice said "One day you will receive power". She didn't know who spoke the words at the time, but looked forward to this promising future before promptly forgetting all about it until many years later, when she realised they were the same words spoken by Jesus regarding the gift of Holy Spirit in Acts 1:8. Although her family left the Roman Catholic Church when Ruth was ten, she later joined her older brother, Jonny, in attending a Christian youth club called Stepping Stones at St Martin's in the Bullring. Jonny developed an obvious respect for the cross, but was tragically killed in a motorcycle accident aged only seventeen. This made Ruth question life after death. A visiting speaker asked the club members if they were good enough to get into Heaven, which concerned Ruth; while she didn't know God, she still hoped for Heaven. At seventeen Ruth's Friend, Grace Penney, brought her to Christ in the back of a minibus on the way home from a school rock-climbing trip. While Ruth has no memory of the actual words Grace spoke to her that day, she knew she'd heard and met with God's arresting truth. Ruth was confirmed and received into the Church of England. She discovered she had the heart of an intercessor-healer, when she saw answered prayer for the healing of a seriously injured friend of Jonny's. But it was five years before Ruth understood the meaning of the cross, during which time she temporarily stopped going to church and lost hope of Heaven, feeling she simply couldn't ever be good enough. However, God never seemed to stop tapping her on the shoulder to say "I'm still here, you know!" She trained to be a Registered General Nurse at St Bartholomew's in London, where eventually her friend Frances Stanton was able to explain that salvation comes through grace, not through works. She suggested that Ruth kneel down to pray to the God who loved her so much that He gave His only Son, to buy back the life she was destined to live in relationship with Him. That day, Holy Spirit seemed to shine not only down on Ruth, but through and out of her. She wept with joy for two days and felt so clean she thought she was incapable of sin for a full two weeks... Then came the lifelong endeavour to know and follow the Lord more deeply and closely. She met her first husband, Graham Jeffery, at St Paul's Church, Robert Adam Street, London, and nursed in Uganda for six months before the wedding. Ruth later became a midwife, Nurse Practitioner and GP Commissioner. They had two beautiful daughters: Joanna and Georgia. During thirty years at St Stephen's Church, Clapham Park, Ruth was a worship leader, prayer minister, administrator and PCC/Deanery Synod Member. Graham very sadly died in 2011. Ruth married Baptist Minister, Rev Ray Scorey, in 2013, moving to Norfolk. Ruth and Ray co-lead Norfolk Healing Rooms, Norfolk School of Prophets and are National Directors for Healing Rooms Scotland. They attend Beacon Community Church in Bacton.

Continue the conversation on FaceBook at the
'Go back to The Garden' page,
where you'll also be updated when the next book is out,
or sign up for free updates at
https://form.jotform.com/232055154751350

Images:

Page	24	*Golden angel wing, courtesy of Fotor Design Templates;*
Page	38	*Tree of Life, courtesy of Picsart;*
Page	76	*Pink spiral, courtesy of kindpng.com*
Page	72	*Picnic, courtesy of Picsart;*
Page	83	*Bucket of tulips, courtesy of Picsart;*
Page	85	*Waterfall, Picsart-edited image (from unattributed photo on www.meets.com);*
Page	86	*Chest of letters, courtesy of Picsart;*
This page		*Sapphire pavement cubic sky tile, courtesy of Fotor Design Templates*

Any non-attributed artwork on the cover and within the body of the manual is by Ruth Scorey, using a blend of doodles, her own photos, digital art and image editing courtesy of Fotor Design Templates and Picsart.

End notes

[i & ii] While beelzebub and satan are personal pronouns, capital letters would assign honour in this manual where none is due

Printed in Great Britain
by Amazon